Praise for *You're Not From Around Here, Are You?*

"Although a white Northerner by birth, Martin Lehfeldt has spent more than half a century in Atlanta, first working for a Black college, always living in a middle-class Black neighborhood, and supporting the city's Black leadership. From his unique vantage point as an activist and an observer, Lehfeldt has written a warm, insightful, often humorous chronicle of his own transformation, and of Atlanta's emergence as the capital of the New South."

—Michael L. Lomax, president, United Negro College Fund

"When New York-born Martin Lehfeldt became an adoptive son of the South, it meant more than an affection for pulled pork sandwiches and warm Januarys. It became a love affair with a place and its people. The South is the environment where Lehfeldt's discerning vision and his talents for storytelling have come to full flower. Those gifts are on vivid display in this book, which is witty, wise, and a sheer delight to read."

—Thomas G. Long, professor emeritus, Emory University

"Martin Lehfeldt's wit and humor are matched by thoughtful observations as he recounts his engagement during the past five decades with people from all walks of life in the South. His stories about Atlanta and the Atlanta University Center help to preserve their history for future generations and offer life lessons that inform and inspire."

—Shirley C. Franklin, former mayor, City of Atlanta

MARTIN LEHFELDT

YOU'RE NOT FROM AROUND HERE, ARE YOU?

Notes from a Naturalized Southerner

BELLE ISLE BOOKS
www.belleislebooks.com

ISBN: 978-1-953021-96-0
LCCN: 2022910761

Project managed by Jenny DeBell

Printed in the United States of America

Published by
Belle Isle Books (an imprint of Brandylane Publishers, Inc.)
5 S. 1st Street
Richmond, Virginia 23219

BELLE ISLE BOOKS
www.belleislebooks.com

belleislebooks.com | brandylanepublishers.com

To my children and grandchildren —
the next custodians of family memories.

TABLE OF CONTENTS

Part Three: Regional Rambling

Part Four: This Land Is Our Land

Acknowledgments

In ways that included gentle encouragement, enthusiastic cheerleading, specific recommendations, keen-eyed proofreading, insightful commentary, and other forms of support, many friends, relatives, and colleagues helped to bring this book to completion This list begins to express but in no way fully captures my thanks.

Grace Ball	Ingrid Kelly
Sue Barnard	Robert Kronley
Bill Bolling	Conrad and Johanna Lehfeldt
Ingrid Briody	Hannah Lehfeldt
Lon Burns	Linda Lehfeldt
Jennifer DeBell	Liz Lehfeldt and David Spaeder
Marian Dickson	Dan and Gwenn Lindsay
Juanita Eber	Handy Lindsey
Jane and David Enniss	Tom Long
Jack Farmer	Grace McCasland
John and Kari Farmer	Linda McCord
Gloria Gayles	Kemie Nix
Greg Gerhard	Kirsten Rambo
David Graham	Mary Lou Romaine
Beth Grashof	Nina Singh
Gary Hauk	Ricky Steele
Kim Henderson	Sheila Taube
Bob Hull	Sally Telford
Robert Hull	Edward Weston
John Inscoe	Jamil Zainaldin
Geraldine Kaylor	

Author's Note

When it came time to produce this book, I decided not to let the rapidly changing dictates of language take all the energy out of my recollections. For the sake of style and variety, I have elected to use Black (capitalized) and African American (unhyphenated) alternately. It is an apolitical decision. Should the hyphenation matter be of special interest, Nobel Prize-winning author, Toni Morrison, wrote, "In this country, American means white. Everyone else has to hyphenate." She chose not to do so, and I am following her lead.

Preface

Dr. Carl Rogers, one of the pioneers in the field of humanistic psychology, considered his early work as a therapist to be a failure. The nondirective counseling technique in which he had been trained simply would not help him to forge a trusting relationship with his clients. In desperation, he finally took a new approach. Dispensing with the distance he had been taught to establish between himself and his clients, he instead shared an experience from his own life with a patient. Rogers was astounded when his openness freed that person to begin confiding in him. This breakthrough led to Roger's formulation of an axiom: that which is most personal is most general.[1] In that spirit, I hope this scattershot collection of personal stories and observations will resonate with readers and trigger their own memories and reflections.

---

[1] Carl R. Rogers, *On Becoming a Person: A Therapist's View of Psychotherapy* (New York: Houghton Mifflin, 1961).

Part One
DISCOVERING MY SOUTH

The Place I Call Home

The ways I love the South go well beyond becoming accustomed to softer speech patterns and discovering a fondness for grits, catfish, fried chicken, barbeque, and collards. However, my affection for the region is not a blind infatuation. I've been wandering around this part of the country long enough now to be acutely aware of its blemishes. Several defects border on the trivial; others are serious shortcomings. The good news is that some of the worst faults—which once seemed hopelessly intractable—show signs of fading and even disappearing.

To take note of that change is to highlight a feature of the South that I love dearly: the contribution of women and men who have chosen to play a part in rescuing the region from its most onerous features and set it on the path to recovery.

More than fifty years ago, I came south on a kind of vocational expedition. That move then steadily expanded into a way of life. The tale of a family exodus evolved into a history of settling in a new land. Now I can no longer imagine living in any other region of the country.

My positive feelings about the South embrace much more than the many pleasures that my booming home city of Atlanta has to offer. I once told my brother-in-law, David, that I could even live in Jackson, Mississippi. That was a brash admission for the once callow, young, white, Northern liberal for whom the very mention of that state used to conjure up images of bigotry, poverty, ignorance, and depravity. But then the Magnolia State (at least portions of it) is also very different than it was when I, with great trepidation, paid my first visit there in mid-1960.

In an early chapter of a book about grant-making foundations in the South[2] that we published in 2019, a colleague and I tried to capture the essence of the South and what sets it apart from other parts of the country. We pointed to a pace of life less frenzied than elsewhere in the country; we highlighted the diverse ecological beauty of the region; we took note of its rich literary tradition. Also on our list of defining characteristics was the South's religious vitality and its unique culinary heritage. Ours, we noted, is the region that gave birth to the blues, gospel, country music, and rock'n'roll. Not all Southerners choose to do so, but the region can also claim with pride that its Black sons and daughters launched a new chapter of the movement for civil rights that brought long-overdue changes to the region and the country.

Linda, my wife of the past thirty-three years, is a native Southerner, and two of my three children still live in the South and are married to Southerners. I deeply resent the aspersions that my friends from elsewhere in the country may cast upon the region of which I now consider myself to be a naturalized citizen. I think I've earned the right to poke fun at or even criticize my fellow Southerners, but other folks better be careful about what they say.

However, despite the sense of belonging I feel in my adopted dwelling place, I must periodically remind myself that I am not truly *of* the South. A simple story will illustrate that point. While I was courting Linda, her maiden aunt came for a visit. During a lunch together while I was absent from the room, Aunt Sarah used the opportunity to comment to her niece, "He seems smitten with you." Linda conceded that my interest in her did indeed seem strong. Then Sarah quickly added, "He's not from around here, is he?"[3] Sarah and I eventually became great friends, but there it was:

---

2 Martin Lehfeldt and Jamil Zainaldin, *The Liberating Promise of Philanthropy* (Atlanta: Storyline Group, 1991).

3 Harry McCool, my East Tennessee-born prosthodontist, is quick to note that where he was raised and in many other parts of the South, the question would be phrased, "You're not from *these here parts. . .*"

the declaration that some combination of genetics and geography had established what would be an enduring difference. So be it.

For many years after the Civil War, one of the South's dominant roles was to serve as a launching pad for hordes of people seeking to escape a war-torn, racism-polluted, economically stagnant, non-air-conditioned region with bad roads. It took nearly a century to staunch and reverse their flight. My arrival occurred during a return migration to the region that started after World War II and accelerated after the passage of critical civil rights legislation during the 1960s.

Since then, what already was a noticeable population shift has swollen into a tidal wave of humanity. Some estimates suggest that within a couple of decades, half of all US residents will be living in the Sunbelt.[4] In the presence of all these newcomers, I feel increasingly less like an interloper and more like a native.

---

4 The name given to the region by Kevin Phillips in *The Emerging Republican Majority* (Princeton University Press, 1969). The term generally encompasses both the southeastern and southwestern states (i.e., Texas, New Mexico, Arizona, and parts of California). However, "my" South consists of Alabama, Arkansas, Florida, Georgia, Kentucky, Louisiana, Mississippi, North Carolina, South Carolina, Tennessee, Virginia, and West Virginia.

A Giant Step

The sun was setting over South Jersey on July 20, 1969, as the Apollo 11 space mission neared its destination. As Michael Collins continued to pilot *Columbia*, the command module, Neil Armstrong and Buzz Aldrin prepared to lower themselves to the face of the moon.

That same hot summer afternoon, my brother and I had loaded a rental van with furnishings from my Hightstown apartment. He drove the truck, and I followed in a car packed with an assortment of household items. We steered onto the New Jersey Turnpike, heading south. Our destination was Atlanta, Georgia. Once the day came to an end and we reached the other side of the Delaware Memorial Bridge, we grabbed a bite to eat and checked into a Howard Johnson motel.

Images of the astronauts flickered across the black and white screen of the television set in our room. The men had steered their module, the *Eagle*, to a safe landing and were now taking their first strides on the lunar surface. To be sure, the venture on which I had embarked that day was no giant leap for mankind. Nonetheless, for this entrenched Yankee to pull up his deep northern roots and relocate to the South was indeed a dramatic move.

The second day after our departure, we rolled into Atlanta to be greeted by my wife and two small children, who had flown down ahead of us. One of my wife's roommates from her Agnes Scott College days had located a three-bedroom unit for us at the attractive Shamrock Gardens apartment complex in the southwest quadrant of the city. My brother returned home, and we began to get settled.

That all took place back when a common characterization of a Yankee by Southerners was a person with a superior attitude who talked too fast and valued efficiency over personal relationships. Further, natives were quick to define a "damn Yankee" as someone who came South with those failings and then stayed. However, stay I did, and what follows is part of that story.

Lest my relocation seem the result of a carefully plotted decision, let me hasten to correct that impression. The real story began five years earlier, as I was preparing to graduate from Union Theological Seminary in New York City. To explain why I was a candidate for a divinity degree would require a much longer story than is needed here. Suffice it to say that I had been "encouraged" since childhood to follow the footsteps of my grandfather and father into the Lutheran ministry. My secret dream was to become a journalist (and I was employed as a newspaper reporter for a while), but I followed the family script and enrolled in a course of theological study.

Along the way, I had developed a love of jazz by frequenting clubs in Greenwich Village; married Anne Russell, a seminary classmate; moved with her into a public housing project; dropped out of seminary for a year to join the staff of a church in Harlem; and, with a partner, formed a small company to generate sorely needed income.

However, after being psychologically freed from this track by my father's untimely death, I decided to abort the mission of preparing for the ministry. (I did fashion a compromise of sorts: I would earn the MDiv degree, but I would not present myself for ordination.) Unfortunately, although liberated from a profession for which I was trained but did not want to pursue, I was then left in the awkward position of being jobless and married to a woman who was pregnant with our first child.

What happened next defies easy explanation. I still don't know whether to credit serendipity, kismet, or the will of an almighty power. As folks are wont to say: "Whatever!" Nonetheless, in rather short order, I applied to and was hired by the Woodrow Wilson

National Fellowship Foundation[5] in Princeton, New Jersey, to direct a new teaching internship program. It would be my responsibility to identify, recruit, and place gifted, mostly white PhD candidates on the faculties of historically Black colleges throughout the South and then coordinate the entire enterprise. The program was generously underwritten by the Rockefeller Foundation.

Several of my cerebrally superior college classmates had received Woodrow Wilson fellowships to prepare for careers in academe, so I already knew of the foundation. However, I was without a clue when it came to the rest of my new job description. My prior exposure to the South consisted of a family camping trip to Virginia when I was seven years old, and I knew virtually nothing about historically Black colleges.

Yet it was to be my relationship with those remarkable institutions during the next four years that provided me with a rare introduction to and perspective on the South. In the final analysis, it was their unique history and potential that attracted me to the region.

---

5 The foundation originated in 1945, when two academic leaders at Princeton University became concerned that young graduate students who had left their studies for military service during World War II would not return to complete their doctoral degrees and enter the teaching profession. They secured some private philanthropy for graduate fellowships to "lure" veterans back to the world of academe. A $100,000 Carnegie Corporation grant to Princeton extended the program modestly but nationally, and it was named to honor the university's former president. Then, in 1957, the Ford Foundation awarded $24.5 million to support 1,000 fellowships each year for five years. The grant was renewed, and during a 15-year period, this venture "encouraged" more than 15,000 of the country's brightest college graduates to enroll in the finest graduate schools and prepare for careers as college professors.

A Southern Treasure

H istorically Black colleges and universities (now commonly referred to as the HBCUs) constitute a unique galaxy in the American educational universe. When I first encountered them, their existence was a mystery to most white folks. Even today, many white Americans would be hard-pressed to name ten of them, or even to give driving directions to the Black colleges in their own communities.

I was similarly ignorant. I happened to know about Hampton Institute[6] in Virginia because a former college roommate had earned his bachelor's degree there. I had heard of Howard, the federally supported university in Washington, DC. I recalled that the Jubilee Singers had once traveled and performed widely to raise funds for Fisk University. That was the sum of my preparedness. And I had never been on a Black college campus.

The student sit-ins of the early 1960s returned these institutions to public awareness.[7] By coincidence, the year I began my new job with the Woodrow Wilson Foundation, their existence was further highlighted by the publication and distribution of a study that identified one hundred and twenty-three HBCUs.[8]

The 150-year history of these remarkable institutions is still

---

6 Became Hampton University in 1984.

7 The first well-publicized protest of this kind occurred on February 1, 1960, when four African American students from A & T College of North Carolina sat down at a Woolworth's lunch counter in Greensboro and requested service.

8 Earl J. McGrath, *The Predominantly Negro Colleges and Universities in Transition*, New York: Teachers College, Columbia University. 1965.

not widely known.[9] When the Civil War came to an end, the state of education throughout the South was deplorable. There were scarcely any public schools for anyone. The wealthy white planters of the antebellum era had enrolled their children in private academies and seminaries or provided them with personal tutors. Very few other white children received schooling, and it was illegal to teach Black slaves to read and write. Such white colleges as did exist were in shambles; Black colleges did not exist at all.

Several ventures set in motion a radical change. In 1865, Congress established the Bureau of Refugees, Freedmen, and Abandoned Lands to help millions of former Black slaves and some poor whites in the South. During its two years of existence, the Freedmen's Bureau opened schools throughout the region. Then, in 1867, George Peabody, an enormously wealthy, Massachusetts-born philanthropist, established a million-dollar fund to establish and/or support public schools across the South, a move that inspired other generous donors to follow suit. Before the end of the nineteenth century, other individuals of great wealth like John Slater, John D. Rockefeller, Anna Jeanes, Sister Katharine Drexel, and Julius Rosenwald played major roles in transforming and advancing still racially segregated Black education throughout the South—from primary school through the university level.

The HBCUs were and are sprinkled across the Southern landscape and beyond, from Cheyney State University and Lincoln University (both close to Philadelphia) to another Lincoln University in Jefferson City, Missouri, and Langston University in Oklahoma. I discovered that Prairie View A&M College was situated at the end of a desolate westward drive from Houston, Texas, on which I saw my first tumbleweed and first armadillo;

---

9 They seem to be rediscovered every few decades. Even as I'm composing this sketch, news accounts abound with stories of multi-million-dollar corporate grants and donations from wealthy white and Black individuals, corporations, and foundations. Reports of this kind would have been sheer fantasy in 1965.

and I learned that one had to leave Arkansas AM&N College in Pine Bluff by early afternoon to catch the last plane leaving Little Rock.

Finding (not identifying, but literally finding) the Black colleges I wanted to visit could be a challenge in those days before satellite-directed travel and before they were listed on road maps or highway signs. I usually rented cars and drove myself to the campuses. The vast interstate network we know today was just beginning to extend across the region; I drove a lot of state highways and county roads through farmland and pine forests to reach the smaller towns in which some of the colleges were situated.

After getting bad or even false information or shrugs from local white folks when I asked for directions, I developed my own navigational system. I would find the courthouse or Confederate memorial on the town square and then drive in ever-widening concentric circles. Once I began seeing more Black faces than white ones (and, in some cases, fewer paved streets and street signs), I knew that I was getting close to my campus destination.[10]

Some of the colleges bore the name of founders and/or donors: Johnson C. Smith, Bethune-Cookman, LeMoyne-Owen. And then there were Talladega and Tougaloo and Tuskegee, which derived their names from geographic territories that white settlers had taken from Native Americans. Protestant denominations played a vital role in the establishment of many of these institutions. The Episcopal Church, with strong encouragement from George Henry Peabody,[11] established three small colleges: St. Augustine's (Raleigh, NC); St. Paul's College (Lawrenceville, VA—closed and sold in 2017); and Voorhees College (Denmark, SC). There also is a single Roman

---

10 The task of finding a historically Black college is now usually routine. Highway and street signs identify their presence, GPS systems furnish directions; all else failing, thoroughfares named after Martin Luther King, Jr. invariably lead to and/or through African American communities in which they often are situated.

11 George Foster Peabody, for whom the famed journalism awards at the University of Georgia are named (no relation to the George Peabody from Massachusetts), was a remarkably progressive Southern leader whose contributions merit more attention by historians.

Catholic institution founded for African American students: Xavier University of Louisiana,[12] in New Orleans. Its faculty included nuns from the Sisters of the Blessed Sacrament whose motherhouse was outside of Philadelphia. The founder of the order, Sister Katharine Drexel (a niece of the renowned banker Anthony Drexel and distantly related to Jacqueline Bouvier) was the heir to a large fortune and recently became only the second American-born individual to be canonized by the Vatican.

Other denominations had their own HBCUs: Lane College in Jackson, TN, established by the Christian (formerly Colored) Methodist Episcopal Church in 1882; Livingstone College, organized in 1879 by leaders of the African Methodist Episcopal Zion Church and placed in Salisbury, NC.; and Oakwood College in Huntsville, AL, founded by the Seventh Day Adventists in 1896.[13]

Among the brightest stars in the constellation of Black colleges was a cluster of six contiguous campuses a mile west of downtown Atlanta. The Atlanta University Center included four undergraduate colleges (Clark, Morehouse, Morris Brown, and Spelman), Atlanta University (a graduate institution with schools of arts and sciences, business, education, library science, and social work) and the Interdenominational Theological Center (itself a federation of Protestant seminaries).[14]

Interestingly, the National Football League was ahead of the rest of the pack when it came to the white rediscovery of the HBCUs. Once the NFL owners, whose teams were then in the North, decided that racial integration would not destroy their enterprise, they began

---

12 Xavier is especially well known for its College of Pharmacy, which has also enrolled white students for many years, and for its nationally ranked success in placing graduates at the country's finest medical schools.

13 I once conducted an evaluative site visit at Oakwood for the United Negro College Fund. As someone who in those days smoked heavily, enjoyed a few shots of bourbon every evening, and preferred real meat to tofu shaped like pork chops, I still think I deserved hardship pay for spending five days on this campus with its clean-living and vegetarian students and faculty.

14 Clark College and Atlanta University merged in 1988 to become Clark Atlanta University.

scouring the football team rosters at the country's major universities for superior Black athletes. They quickly learned that the pool was limited; those universities were themselves new to the racial integration game. The "Brud" Hollands of the world were in short supply,[15] and Holland declined the chance to play pro ball.

Then, the recruiters found the HBCUs. One favorite source of talent was Grambling College in rural Louisiana; its legendary coach, Eddie Robinson, trained and sent a steady stream of players to the pros. Another was Florida A&M in Tallahassee, whose "Rattlers" were coached by Jake Gaither—another giant in Black football circles. Other historically Black state colleges[16] also were sources of professional football talent.

But smaller and private Black colleges yielded prospects too. Elijah Pitts, the powerful running back of the Green Bay Packers, came from Philander Smith College. Whenever I heard a sports broadcaster call out his name, I could picture that small United Methodist institution (named after a generous white donor from the Chicago area), perched on a hill overlooking the then dusty and sleepy downtown area of Little Rock, the capital of Arkansas.

That recruitment pattern has changed. Now and then, a story will appear in the sports section of the newspaper about a young man from an HBCU being drafted by a professional football team. However, it's much more typical now for a gifted Black athlete to graduate from high school, be recruited by a formerly segregated Southern university, and then find his way from there to the professional leagues.

---

15 Jerome H. (Brud) Holland was the first African American to play football at Cornell University and was named an All-American in 1937 and 1938. He received his PhD from the University of Pennsylvania and became president of historically Black Delaware State College before going on to the presidency of Hampton Institute. In 1970, President Richard Nixon appointed him Ambassador to Sweden. One of my strongest memories of Brud involves him coming upon me at the registration desk for a conference in Washington, DC, and greeting me with a friendly backslap that knocked me several feet across the lobby.

16 Including Arkansas AM&N, Alabama A&M and Alabama State, Albany State, Fort Valley State, Savannah State, Kentucky State, Alcorn A&M, Jackson State, A&T of North Carolina, Southern University in Louisiana, South Carolina State, Tennessee State A&I, Virginia State, and Norfolk State.

Today, there are still approximately seventy historically Black colleges and universities, both private and public, in the United States. Most of the survivors are accredited, although several are hanging on to life by their fingernails. A couple of medical and law schools, and a small handful of theological seminaries share the same lineage.

The United Negro College Fund, founded in 1944, includes thirty-seven private Black member institutions for which it conducts an annual campaign. For many years, "A Mind Is a Terrible Thing to Waste" was one of the best-known fundraising slogans in the country. Collectively, the private and public historically Black colleges and universities have been one of the greatest, albeit hidden, treasures of the South.

Welcome to the South

O ne of my early working trips to the South also was my first visit to Florida in 1966. It brought me to Daytona Beach for a visit to Bethune-Cookman College. From there I intended to drive to Gainesville for a visit with a former college roommate on the University of Florida faculty, and then continue by plane to a meeting in New Orleans.

Travel in those days was a bit different than it is now. One had no access to a GPS. We planned our trips and made our way around the country with the assistance of devices called road maps. They were intricately folded paper charts produced by oil companies and distributed for free at places called filling stations which sold the petroleum products of those companies. Those stations were staffed by men in uniforms who dispensed gasoline from pumps. Often, they also washed the windshields of customers' cars and checked the oil level of their engines. Some of them could repair flat tires, tune and change spark plugs, and replace fan belts.

When I consulted my Esso map of Florida that Saturday morning, I could not identify a direct route from Daytona to Gainesville. However, a dotted line between the two municipalities indicated that a road might be in the planning stages. When I sought the advice of the good ol' boy who filled my car's gas tank, he informed me that a friend of his had driven that route the day before.

Emboldened by this news, I set forth on my journey. I found the cut off to the "dotted line" highway with no difficulty and headed west on a newly paved road. I was soon in the heart of rural Florida. There wasn't a neon sign or any other evidence of commercial intrusion to be seen. A couple of bored-looking, long-horned cattle in a nearby field reinforced the tranquil setting. It was a beautiful day. The sun above me shone brightly; the sky was a radiant blue. Traffic was light and then non-existent. I would certainly be in Gainesville earlier than expected. Life was good.

My reveries were interrupted when I noticed ahead of me that the asphalt on which I was riding would soon come to an end. Beyond that point the road appeared clear and graded, but it was not paved. I lowered my speed, drove to the edge of the asphalt, and stopped. Clearly, I was facing a simple choice: either continue, or turn back and find another way.

I took a bit of comfort from the knowledge that the garage attendant's friend allegedly had come this way the day before. I also did not relish the notion of having to retrace my route and locate another, lengthier way to my destination. What was the worst that could happen if I were to continue? I soon found out.

It was beginning to dawn on me that the area through which I was driving must have been hit by heavy rains before my arrival. As I slowly edged my way onto the flattened soil, the car's rear tires began spinning in place. They finally lost all traction as my vehicle slowly settled into what I now realized was simply deep, thick mud.

From my stranded position I could see a drainage canal several yards away in which was slowly moving what I can only describe as—I'm not kidding—a large reptile. (I had been an English major in college; I didn't know how to distinguish an alligator from a crocodile.) It continued slowly swimming away from me. With that threat removed, I could begin planning. I pushed the car door open just enough for me to squeeze out—and to step knee-deep into the sticky muck.

About thirty feet ahead of me was another stretch of road. It wasn't paved, but it had been leveled and covered with gravel. If I could reach it, I'd be in good shape. *If.* . . . It might as well have been a mile away. I was not going to get there without assistance.

The large amphibian was out of sight. I was feeling very alone. (Remember, this was in the mid-1960s; cell phones were still a figment of someone's imagination.) I smoked a few cigarettes and mopped my sweaty head with a handkerchief.

At long last I heard the welcome sound of a vehicle approaching. Help seemed to be at hand—if one could define rescue as four inebriated yahoos in a beat-up, all-terrain vehicle. When they stopped at the end of the graded road ahead of me, the fellow in the front passenger seat stood up and hollered, "Hey, good buddy!" and then unnecessarily asked, "You stuck?"

Neither of us had a rope or chain, so the relief squad decided, with great whoops of merriment and genial profanity, that they were going to push me backward out of the mud. They instructed me to get back behind the wheel and then proceeded to drive straight toward me. They were moving slowly, but not slowly enough. I could hear my front bumper crumple before the Jeep driver accelerated. My vehicle moved an inch or two, but my angels of mercy clearly didn't have the power to dislodge me.

After a few more attempts, they backed onto firmer ground and agreed that they had done all they could. With cries of "Hang in there!" and "Good luck, pal!" they disappeared in the direction from which they had come. I was left alone again in the sweltering silence with a car up to its axles in mud—and no sign of other human life. I smoked a few more cigarettes, convinced myself that the birds in those nearby trees were not buzzards, and pondered my plight.

The next vehicle that finally appeared was a large pick-up truck. A middle-aged man sat behind the steering wheel on a bench seat with his wife and small child beside him. He climbed out, surveyed the situation, and then announced, "I'm gonna pull you out. Stay there." He turned his truck around and backed it to the edge of the graded area. After fastening one end of a long chain to a trailer hitch, he waded in his boots through the mud and secured the other end somewhere under the front of my sedan. "Get behind your wheel," he instructed. He returned to his truck, slipped it into low gear, and ever so slowly pulled me free of the mire. When the operation was complete, he refused to let me pay him and drove away.

I was free. The Lord had planted my feet on higher ground.

I made my way to a puddle by the side of the road to rinse off my muddy hands. As I bent over, my trousers split up the back. It was time for a round of profound and inventive cursing.

The traffic increased as I pulled into Gainesville an hour or so later. Then it became much heavier. It dawned on me that I had managed to arrive shortly before kickoff time at a homecoming weekend football game. The Gators were playing, and seemingly half of the state's population had shown up to watch them. I had my friend's address, but I didn't have directions. (As already noted, global positioning systems were still in our future.) It took a while, but I maneuvered my vehicle out of the congestion. My search for a pay telephone (a popular communications device in those days) yielded one in a filling station parking lot. A pair of geezers in bib overalls and baseball caps seated on a bench in front of the station watched me impassively as I climbed from the car and shuffled awkwardly in my mud-stained and split trousers to the phone to call for directions to my friend's home.

The next afternoon, after my Gainesville visit, I parked the filthy and slightly damaged rental vehicle in a lot near the Jacksonville airport, as far from sight of the office as possible to avoid questioning, turned in the keys, and climbed into the shuttle van. A few hours later I checked into the Hotel Monteleone on the edge of the French Quarter in New Orleans, more than ready for a stiff drink at its revolving Carousel Bar.

Exporting Culture

The Teaching Internship Program periodically generated some interesting programmatic twists. For example, one of our English instructors advanced the notion that it might be of value to put a team of poets on the road to conduct readings and to lead seminars at the HBCUs served by the teaching interns. What can I say? It was the sixties, and the idea was able to attract the necessary funding. With financial support assured, we began identifying possible participants.

Soon thereafter, I climbed aboard a train from Princeton Junction to New York City with Hans Rosenhaupt, the foundation's president, and then hailed a cab from Penn Station to the Chelsea Hotel on West Twenty-Third Street.

The Chelsea, with its ornate, wrought-iron balconies on the front of the building, had been the residence of many legendary writers and artists over the years. Mark Twain, Virgil Thomson, Jackson Pollock, Arthur Miller, Dylan Thomas, Bette Midler, and Allen Ginsberg were just a few of the luminaries on the guest list. The hotel's bohemian reputation would continue into the 1970s. Leonard Cohen had an affair with Janis Joplin there and wrote at least one song about it. Sid Vicious, he of the Sex Pistols, would shoot his girlfriend to death on the premises and then try to kill himself.

The atmosphere was decidedly calmer the afternoon we arrived at the hotel. We joined a collection of mild-mannered, established and emerging poets, both white and Black: Donald Hall, Galway Kinnell, Isabella Gardner, Milton Kessler, Donald Finkel, A. B. Spellman, Jay Wright.

The hospitality arrangements were austere. We didn't have enough chairs, so most of us sat on the floor, leaning against the walls, in a sparsely furnished living room. The poets primarily wore jeans and other casual garb; Hans and I were in suits and ties, but we discarded our jackets. Beverage containers consisted of plastic cups and mismatched glass tumblers. The single tray of ice cubes from the refrigerator was insufficient for our purposes, so we sipped warm vodka and shared ideas as we planned our literary invasion of the South.

☾☾☾☾

PS: No one from the foundation staff accompanied the poets on their visits, and none of the teaching interns, to my knowledge, prepared written reports. However, when this intersectional cultural foray came to an end, oral accounts by the poets and others declared it to be a success. To my knowledge, in addition to not being recorded, it was never repeated.

Indirect Benefits

The salary I received from the foundation was by no means excessive, but the compensation package included some attractive "perks." A major benefit was related to the extensive air travel required of me. Upon my arrival in Princeton, the foundation's business manager issued me a wad of credit cards, and another colleague explained that it was customary for the program staff to fly first class.

One particularly enjoyable trip that I generally took twice a year during the late 1960s was a late afternoon flight from Newark to Los Angeles. My secretary would book me a first-class seat in the smoking section. Then, the day before departure, a United Airlines representative would call to inquire whether Mr. Lehfeldt would prefer the steak or the lobster as his main course.

Those of us destined for the front of the plane received the initial boarding call. Finding my seat was no challenge. It was marked with a bright red placard on which my name was embossed in gold lettering. If there were any further questions about where I was to sit, on the armrest was a pack of similarly labeled matches. After a stewardess (then the name for a member of the all-female ranks of flight attendants) took my jacket (we wore suits and ties when we traveled), she would ask me for my aperitif preference: champagne? a mimosa? something stronger? If necessary, that drink would be replenished until the pilot announced his readiness to take off.

Then came cocktails and snacks. A specialty on United was the dish of macadamia nuts for each first-class passenger. Then wine selections. Then salad. Then the main course, everything served with cloth napkins and silverware and a continuing stream of cabernet sauvignon or chardonnay. It was a long flight, so there was still time to sip Courvoisier after dessert. I periodically felt some guilt for my participation in this pampered travel style, but another sip of Cognac usually was sufficient to stifle that sensation.

Those days of self-indulgence are long gone, but my vivid memories of them still can crease my face with a broad smile. I miss that time of privilege, separated by a curtain from the unwashed masses back in steerage.

However, another state of mind soon replaced my superior attitude after that life of generous travel budgets came to an end. Since then, finding myself wedged into a narrow seat near the back of a plane, only a few rows from the rear lavatory, my thoughts swiftly turn toward revolution. These days I instead contemplate the overthrow of those arrogant, domineering plutocrats/those fat-assed capitalist pigs on the other side of the curtain at the front of the aircraft (one of them probably in MY seat).

❧❧❧❧

During my tenure at the foundation, my responsibilities included helping to keep the teaching internship program funded. That task essentially involved composing written requests to the Rockefeller Foundation—the initial backer of our program—for grant renewals and following up with face-to-face discussions. It was a most genteel process that included periodic trips to New York for catered luncheons in the exquisitely furnished and hushed offices of the foundation officials who supported and monitored our work.

The Rockefeller vice president with whom we most often met resembled the Hollywood stereotype of a foundation officer. He was tall and erect, gray-haired, courtly, and wore well-tailored dark suits. He asked good questions, listened politely to the answers, and exuded an air of wisdom and rectitude. As I came to discover, in those days, New York's many foundations were staffed by other similar older white males and were often headed by distinguished former college presidents and high-ranking government officials.

During my first visit to the Rockefeller Foundation, in (what else?) a Rockefeller Center building on Fifth Avenue, Dean Rusk, the Foundation's president and later Secretary of State under both presidents Kennedy and Johnson, stepped off an elevator with a man and woman whom he introduced to us as Ferdinand and Imelda Marcos. (We didn't know about her collection of shoes in those days, so I didn't stare at her feet.)

For the most part, the world of organized philanthropy today is a different realm than the one I've been describing. Soon after, it went through an intensive period of scrutiny by Congress. Some elected officials with a populist bent wanted to force the liquidation of all foundations. That didn't happen, but the Tax Reform Act of 1969 got the attention of the field. Foundations today, with notable exceptions, are more circumspect about the way they spend their money on themselves.

Nonetheless, I was properly awed by my introduction to what then was the stratosphere of philanthropy. I think I also knew instinctively that I probably shouldn't aspire to that kind of professional life. As fate would have it, my hunch was correct.

Wanting to Make a Difference

Many of my travels through the South required that I first fly to Atlanta—a city I was getting to know and enjoy. I proposed to my boss that the foundation let me relocate my office there. When he could find no merit in that suggestion, I entered a period of restlessness. I felt ready for a change and explored several other job possibilities. Deep down, though, my strongest inclination was to follow the lead of the young professors whom I had been dispatching to the South. I felt that I too could make a difference in that setting. Unfortunately, that desire faced a major impediment: I didn't have the academic credentials needed to join a college faculty.

The foundation had recently established a new fellowship program for Black veterans of military service that I was helping to direct. During a trip to Atlanta to interview candidates,[17] I asked Edward Brantley, Vice President of Clark College and one of my search committee members, whether he knew of any job openings in the Atlanta University Center. He told me that his institution was looking for a development officer.[18] I no longer remember whether I waited until my return to Princeton, but I quickly made it clear to him that I was interested in becoming a candidate.

What I knew about fundraising could have been captured in writing on the back of a postage stamp. Perhaps it was because I had been employed by something that called itself a foundation—and foundations reputedly had money and gave it away—that I got the

---

17 William Harvey, current president of Hampton University, was among the first candidates to receive one of these Martin Luther King, Jr. Graduate Fellowships.

18 The polite term for a fundraiser.

job. It may also have had to do with my willingness to take a thirty percent pay cut. Anyway, I became Clark's first vice president for development and the school's first white administrator since its earliest days. It would become my responsibility to guide the design and coordination of the college's asset building program.

My wife at the time, Anne, liked the idea of returning to Atlanta. A few of her classmates and close friends from nearby Agnes Scott College were still in the area. Our children were too young to know the difference. We bid Princeton goodbye and set off on a new adventure.

My early days on the job were not especially auspicious. It soon became apparent that no one had thought through exactly what I was supposed to be doing. I was awarded the use of one-sixth of a sub-divided trailer. It contained a battered desk, a swivel chair, and a used electric typewriter.

A grant from the Mary Reynolds Babcock Foundation of Winston-Salem, North Carolina, underwrote my cruelly constrained salary. I spent the first year going to meetings, learning more about the college, becoming acquainted with board members, and composing grant requests to foundations. What got me through until my skills improved were entrepreneurial instincts, better-than-average writing skills, a visionary college president, and an imaginative fundraising consultant.[19]

The next period of my life would be a swirling period of change and discovery. My eight-year union with Anne came to an end. I subsequently married Ann Ashford, one of her college roommates. My new wife and I joined Central Presbyterian Church and began raising my two children. Through a series of professional adventures and personal escapades, I learned a lot about my newly adopted region, about my colleagues, friends, and neighbors, about fundrais-

---

19 Irving Warner, author of *The Art of Fund Raising*. I first met Irving (since deceased) when my first wife was his secretary in New York while he was organizing a major fundraising event. Irving, who was based in Los Angeles, became a close friend and one of our daughter's godparents. He was experienced, brash, opinionated, funny, inventive, and a wonderful mentor. When we began organizing Clark College's first capital campaign, I immediately called upon him for assistance.

ing, and about myself. Perhaps the strongest indicator that I might be destined to remain in the South came when I declined two separate offers to join the development staff of my college alma mater. I seemed to be hooked on my new habitat.

Part Two
PUTTING DOWN ROOTS

Mrs. Crane

After my first wife and I drew the curtain on eight years of marriage, I received custody of our two very young children. As someone with a full-time job, I was going to need help on the home front. I advertised for a children's caretaker who could come early and stay until supper five days a week.

When I began interviewing applicants for the position, I had no idea what questions I should be asking. Aside from periodic babysitters, our tots had never been left with anyone except grandparents—and those folks were hundreds of miles away in the North Country. What did I need to know about these caretakers, whose purpose was to function as a surrogate parent? What skills should they have? I guessed that it might be helpful if they had experienced motherhood themselves. I had to face it, though: I was flying blind and relying on pure intuition.

Why did I hire Mrs. Crane? I still don't know for certain. She was a quiet, brown-skinned, middle-aged woman with a soft voice and a gentle smile. As she sat on the living room sofa in my apartment, her thighs and breasts formed that kind of cushioned refuge into which a small child would want to climb for comfort.

I had by then lived in the South long enough to know some of the social amenities. One of them was that white families called African American domestic help by their first names. From the start, though, Martin Lehfeldt, the great white liberal reformer from the North, would have none of that. He and his children would address their new employee by her last name. And so, to us she was Mrs. Crane. Native Southerners, both white and Black, smiled pityingly at this foolish breach of custom, but the name stuck. Mrs. Crane may have been a bit discomfited by my attempt to liberate her, but she said nothing.

The day of her interview, Mrs. Crane wore a dress with a sweater draped over her shoulders. I cannot remember a time thereafter, though, when she didn't appear at our door in a white uniform dress. She looked like her counterparts whom I had seen with children on the north side of town. I think it was her way of making it clear to everyone that she was a professional. Having won the nomenclature battle, I wasn't about to push my luck by tackling housekeeper dress codes.

I did make one other attempt to turn Mrs. Crane into a non-conformist of sorts. She was satisfied with what I paid her, but she had no intention of going along with my suggestion that I also put money into a Social Security account for her. She listened carefully as I championed the importance of retirement savings and then politely but firmly replied, "I'll take cash."

She didn't have a car. One of her children or other relatives usually brought her to work and picked her up at the end of the day. She never failed to show up. One day, when she couldn't get a ride, she commandeered a beat-up jalopy and drove herself to Shamrock Gardens. I doubt that she had a valid driver's license, but I didn't ask.

Even after a year of this relationship, I didn't have an especially precise idea of what happened during my daily absence. Neighbors reported to me that they had seen Mrs. Crane, escorted by the children, taking dirty clothes to the apartment complex's laundromat. She obviously fixed lunch, kept the place clean, and played with Liz and Conrad. All I know is that when I returned home from work in the evening, the clean apartment radiated calm, it smelled of freshly ironed clothing, the television set was not blaring, and the "chirrn" (as she called them) were bathed, in their pajamas, and playing quietly with their toys on the living room carpet. All was right with the world. I would fix supper, put the children to bed, and we would have made it through another day.

The experience lasted only a year or so until I found my way back into the state of matrimony, but one temporary bachelor father remains eternally grateful for all that Mrs. Crane meant to our family.

The Aroma of Ambition: Atlanta in 1969

I had visited Atlanta regularly during the previous four years and changed planes there many more times. My passages through the new airport were frequent enough that a couple of the bartenders in one of the lounges even remembered my first name.

The Atlanta of 1969 in which I chose to settle bore only faint resemblance to the towering cityscape that today marches for miles along the Peachtree Street ridge or the metropolis that now oozes, unchecked, into an ever-growing collection of neighboring counties. However, its architecture and construction already emitted the deep aroma of ambition. That sprawling airport, a sparkling stadium, architect John Portman's steadily expanding downtown complex of gleaming white office towers, highlighted by the soaring, open atrium of the Regency Hyatt House and the Polaris Lounge—which people stood in line for blocks to visit or simply gape at. these and other signals made it clear that my new hometown was on the move.[20]

The dark side of all this feverish construction was Atlanta's zest for demolition. The "old" Equitable Building on Edgewood

---

20 Even before embarking upon his massive downtown development, Portman had designed Greenbriar Mall, the city's third enclosed shopping center, which opened in 1965. A short drive from our new apartment, it offered the benefits of two major department stores, a Woolworth's, a well-stocked liquor store, a Delta Air Lines ticket counter, a restaurant, a movie theater, and a branch of the Atlanta Public Library. It was also in that mall that Truett Cathy, the founder of Chick-fil-A, who was offering chicken sandwiches at his Dwarf House in nearby Hapeville, put his first outlet in 1967.

Avenue was gone; a contract had been signed for the destruction of the beaux arts Terminal Station; major hotels (the Kimbell House, the Dinkler Plaza) and theaters like Loew's were disappearing. The Carnegie Library would soon be just a memory. Within a few years, only a magnificent eruption of citizen protest would save the once-grand-but-now-seedy Fox Theatre from annihilation. The partner of Atlanta's rising phoenix was the wrecking ball.

One delightful piece of restoration that fought the destructive trend was a development called Underground Atlanta. Years earlier, the treacherous crush of trains and streetcars had rendered downtown streets almost impassable. The city's response to the congestion was to build viaducts across them. Businesses that faced those streets moved their operations to the second floor and either used their original first floors for storage or closed them. What amounted to a twelve-acre section of property was almost forgotten (although speakeasies allegedly flourished there during Prohibition). Construction work on a new rapid rail system uncovered an architectural time capsule filled with a treasure trove of beautiful building fronts with ornate carving, ironwork, and other decorative touches.

Entrepreneurship, the extension of favorable drinking laws, and a growing city soon led to the establishment, also in 1969, of a new entertainment district. Both Atlantans and tourists flocked to enjoy the vitality and variety of Underground Atlanta's exciting array of shops, restaurants, and clubs with live music.[21]

The Atlanta Braves baseball franchise had come from Milwaukee in 1966 and would win its division championship by 1969. Mayor Ivan Allen, III, a powerful booster of that move, famously said that having a professional sports franchise was the only way he knew to assure that his city's name would appear in the national news every day.

---

21 Unfortunately, within a decade, white flight, relaxed drinking laws in the suburban counties, the arrival of a criminal element, poor public safety, and other factors led to the almost complete dissolution of what should have continued as a major showcase for Atlanta. It was essentially abandoned until the twenty-first century, and its future remains a question mark.

The Memorial Arts Center had opened in 1968. It was a tribute to the many art patrons who had died in the 1962 plane crash at Orly Airport in France, thereby establishing a prominent place for the arts in Atlanta's future. It initially housed the High Museum of Art, the Alliance Theater, the Atlanta Symphony Orchestra, and the Atlanta College of Art.

A few of the mercantile chains now had branches on the outskirts of the city (most notably Lenox Square), but one could still go shopping downtown at Rich's and Davison's and Kessler's. Indeed, the racially segregated Nancy Hanks[22] train continued to convey folks from Savannah to Atlanta (a six-hour run each way) for an afternoon of shopping.

All the major law firms and accounting partnerships were also downtown. Dominating the crowded Five Points area were the city's first skyscrapers: Fulton National Bank, Bank of Georgia, First National Bank, and the new Equitable Building. (Within a few years, Robert Woodruff, Coca-Cola's legendary former chairman, would anonymously purchase four acres of this cramped urban real estate and underwrite its conversion into a beautiful park.) Elsewhere downtown were the government buildings: the federal courthouse, the state capital buildings, the county courthouse, and City Hall.

East of the white downtown was the Sweet Auburn commercial district, dominated by the Atlanta Life Insurance Company but also including a variety of attorney and physician practices, as well as the *Atlanta Daily World*, stores, nightclubs, barbershops, a couple of motels, Citizens Trust Bank, and the City Market, where one butcher said they sold "every part of the pig except the squeal."

Another pocket of Black enterprise was the Hunter Street corridor that began downtown and headed west. Ralph David Abernathy's church, West Hunter Street Baptist, stood there, as well as the offices and shops of Black professionals, like the renowned at-

---

22 Named for a famous racehorse (an undefeated standardbred trotter mare from Kentucky) that in turn had been named for Abraham Lincoln's mother (for reasons I have yet to discover).

torney, Donald Hollowell.[23] Best known was Paschal's, a restaurant and gathering place that had become the informal headquarters of the Civil Rights Movement. James and Robert Paschal had never paid attention to racial segregation laws and ordinances, and their establishment was one of the few places in Atlanta where African Americans and white people could meet both to fraternize and to plan. It didn't hurt its popularity that Robert Paschal's recipe for fried chicken was considered by many to be the best in town. Next to the restaurant the brothers also established La Carousel Lounge, the city's best jazz club, in a nearly pitch-Black basement space where nationally known artists as well as local musicians performed regularly.

During my many travels through Atlanta, I had initially stayed in a variety of downtown hotels, but that pattern changed after the Paschals constructed a 120-room hotel above their restaurant in 1967. The rooms were large, the rates were reasonable, the food was good, and the staff was friendly. I also quickly discovered that I seldom needed to schedule appointments with the academics from the nearby Atlanta University Center with whom I wanted to visit. All that was needed was to grab a seat at one of the booths in the front room of the restaurant at about eight o'clock in the morning. Invariably, most of the folks I wanted to meet would wander through, as would a gaggle of other ordinary people and celebrities. By late morning, Ms. Ora Belle Sherman, the glamorous and ageless hostess, would come by, gushing a welcome and an invitation to stay for lunch.

Downtown Atlanta still gave the appearance of being a religious as well as commercial and civic citadel. Several white churches had resisted the temptation to flee Capitol Hill: Central Presbyterian, Trinity United Methodist, and the Shrine of the Immaculate Conception continued to hunker beneath the shadow of the capi-

---

23 Some twenty years later, Marvin Arrington, Sr. commissioned me to write Hollowell's biography. Louise Hollowell and Martin Lehfeldt, *The Sacred Call: A Tribute to Donald L. Hollowell*, forward by Vernon E. Jordan, Jr., (Winter Park, Florida: Four-G Publishers, Inc., 1997).

tol's gold-sheathed dome. The hulking Baptist Tabernacle stood on Luckie Street, First United Methodist was on Peachtree Street, and St. Luke's Episcopal Church and Sacred Heart Catholic Church were a few blocks farther north. Given its denomination's abolitionist heritage, the historically African American First Congregational Church fittingly occupied a position on Courtland Street between the formerly all-Black Old Fourth Ward and white Atlanta.

Other churches had many years earlier moved to, or resettled in, what had been the northern edge of the city but already was being called "Midtown": North Avenue Presbyterian, All Saints Episcopal, Lutheran Church of the Redeemer, First Baptist, and St. Mark United Methodist.

Even though African Americans were beginning to establish residence in other sections of the city, many of their church memberships remained at First Congregational, Ebenezer Baptist, Wheat Street Baptist, Big Bethel A.M.E., and Butler Street C.M.E. in the Old Fourth Ward. On the edges of the Atlanta University Center, Friendship Baptist, Central United Methodist, and Warren Memorial United Methodist all had thriving memberships. It seemed possible to throw a stone in any direction from any corner in the city and hit a white or Black Baptist church—from storefront chapels to spire-topped sanctuaries.

In 1969, the year of my arrival, Johnson C. Smith Theological Seminary—which had been a division of the university with the same name in Charlotte—relocated to Atlanta with a handful of students and became the fifth member of the Interdenominational Theological Center.

The broad view credited strong white male business leaders and wise mayors with having steered Atlanta through the turmoil of racial conflict that began during the early 1960s and led to violence in other Southern cities. It was, after all, "the city too busy to hate," a kind of spiritualizing axiom to describe a city of white and Black hustlers who loved to turn a buck. And certainly, its relatively peaceful transition through the Civil Rights Movement days would not have occurred without those moderate white leaders.

Often overlooked, or at least downplayed, was the role of their Black counterparts, who sat across the table from these white power brokers during critical negotiations and deal making. Many of them were products of the institutions that constituted the Atlanta University Center. They were easily the equals of, if not educationally superior to, their fellow Caucasian leaders. Among the names that immediately flash to mind is that of the remarkable Dr. Benjamin E. Mays, the former President of Morehouse College and mentor of Martin Luther King, Jr., who went on to become the first African American chairman of the Atlanta School Board.

Memories of Dr. Martin Luther King's assassination the year before continued to permeate the otherwise civic atmosphere. His body still rested south of the city at Southview Cemetery on Jonesboro Road, in the graveyard established by African Americans before the beginning of the twentieth century. Meanwhile, his widow and former colleagues planned the Martin Luther King, Jr. Center for Nonviolent Social Change (and a more public burial place) on Auburn Avenue. Very important for the future, the city had made it through King's funeral without significant racial upheaval, and the signs pointed towards continued non-violent negotiations in race relations in honor of Dr. King's philosophy.

Also, the year before my arrival, a small cadre of anti-establishment young people launched *The Great Speckled Bird*, a countercultural newspaper whose first edition included an attack on the revered Ralph McGill for his support of U.S. policy toward Vietnam. The paper's editorial policy might well have been "Nothing is sacred."

Another development of major regional significance occurred the year I arrived. In response to a nationwide assault by the U.S. Congress on grant-making foundations, and with leadership from William Archie, a North Carolina foundation leader, and several of Atlanta's philanthropic figures, the Southeastern Council of Foundations came into being.[24]

---

24 Archie, who had once been Emory University's Dean of Arts and Sciences, was the Executive Director of the Mary Reynolds Babcock Foundation in Winston-Salem, the same organization that first paid my salary at Clark College. Among his

Political change also was coming fast on the heels of economic acceleration and social shifts. The year before I arrived in Atlanta, Maynard Jackson, a smart, brash Morehouse graduate with impeccable family credentials and an only slightly used law degree, decided to run for public office. Not content with seeking a seat in the General Assembly[25] as more than a few other AU Center alumni had done, the ambitious Jackson set his sights high. He was going to challenge Herman Talmadge, former Georgia Governor and well-entrenched U.S. Senator. Of course, Jackson lost the contest; the Millennium would be delayed a bit longer. But when he carried the election within Atlanta's city limits, people sat up and took notice.

---

co-founders were Boisfeuillet Jones, President of the Emily and Ernest Woodruff Foundation, and John Griffin, Executive Director of the Southern Education Foundation, both based in Atlanta. Legal counsel to the venture was Randolph Thrower, the Atlanta attorney who was President Richard Nixon's Commissioner of the Internal Revenue Service and later was fired when he objected to the administration's plan to use tax audits to punish its "enemies." Twenty-nine years later, I was honored to become the first non-Southern President of the SECF.

25 In 1962, State Senator Leroy Johnson (who died in 2019) became the first African American elected to the legislature since Reconstruction and took his seat in 1963. Two years later, Julian Bond and seven other African Americans were elected to the Georgia House of Representatives.

The School on a Hill
(A Tribute to Vivian W. Henderson)

There's a school on a hill
That we love good and true,
With a love that enlightens
Our souls through and through:
'Tis the shrine of a race and
'Tis owned by a king,
And dear to our hearts
Are the praises we sing.

Oh! We love every building
That stands on the hill,
And we love e'en the trees
Wav'ring, whispering still
And oft to our dear
Alma Mater we hark
Oh! God bless you and keep you,
Our dear old Clark.

The School on a Hill was the hymn of Clark College[26] in Atlanta, which hired me as its vice president for development in 1969. If the final refrain seems vaguely familiar, that's because a portion of the lyrics and the entire melody were lifted directly from an Irish American show tune written in 1910.[27]

---

26 Now Clark Atlanta University.

27 Composed by Ernest Ball, who also created the tune for "When Irish Eyes Are Smiling."

When Clarence Coleman, the dapper and proud Black executive director of the Atlanta Urban League and president of the Clark National Alumni Association in those days, would lock arms with me to sing the alma mater, he would glance in my direction, roll his eyes, and whisper in disbelief, "Mother Machree?"

One reference in the song initially baffled me—the one about the college's elevation. The campus on which I came to work dipped here and there, but all in all, it seemed to rest upon reasonably flat terrain. A knowledgeable alumna eventually explained to me that Clark had once been situated south of the city. Assisted by that prompt, I remembered seeing a cluster of buildings that overlooked the east side of the new interstate the first time I drove into Atlanta from the airport. As I came to learn, the largest of them, an impressive late Gothic Revival structure that included a large chapel, was Leete Hall—the dominant building on the campus of the "old" Clark.[28]

Clark built an entirely new campus adjacent to Atlanta University, Morehouse College, and Spelman College during the early 1940s. Later joined by Morris Brown College and the Interdenominational Theological Center, the complex became known as the Atlanta University Center.

The alumni association, like a good portion of Clark, was in disarray when Vivian W. Henderson arrived to become its president in 1965. He recounted the story of his introduction to that organization this way: "When I was invited to speak to the group at homecoming during my first year at Clark, I showed up expecting to address an auditorium full of graduates. I got there early and found about fifteen people all electing each other as officers. *Lord,* I thought, *we need some help bad!*"

As I would learn from him and others, that was to be among the least of his worries. One of his early discoveries was that "dear old Clark," far from enjoying the financial stability that the search com-

---

28 *http://georgiaencyclopedia.org/articles/education//clark-atlanta-university*; see also Campus Heritage Plan of Clark Atlanta University, prepared by Beth Grashop for Clement & Wynn, Program Mangers, March 2007.

mittee had described to him, was teetering on the brink of bankrupt-
cy. Without complaint, he set out to repair the damage.

Before all the records and memories disappear, I hope that
someone will write a complete biography of this remarkable leader who, during his decade-long presidency, transformed an average
undergraduate institution into one of the leading historically Black
colleges in the country. For now, here is my long overdue tribute to
him.

Let the record show that Vivian W. Henderson was born in
Bristol, Tennessee, graduated from North Carolina College in
Durham, served in the U.S. Army, received an MBA in 1947, and by
1952 had earned his doctorate in labor economics at the University
of Iowa. He taught briefly at his undergraduate alma mater and at
Prairie View A&M College in Texas before joining the faculty of the
prestigious Fisk University in Nashville. Four years before I arrived,
Clark snatched him up and brought him to Atlanta along with his
lovely wife, Anna, and four young children.

Unlike many of his predecessors and colleagues, Henderson's
universe was far broader than the narrow ecclesiastical and professional circles in which they had been raised and shaped. He was both
a scholar and an activist. His pioneering economic research (including his article titled "Negro Colleges Face the Future") and his innate
leadership skills led to his involvement with more local, state, regional, and national councils, commissions, and organizations than I can
list here. That background immersed him in major public issues, put
him in peer relationships with influential people, and armed him
with great expectations.

Since his authorship of pioneering labor and employment studies in Nashville and elsewhere, one of Henderson's passions had been
to move more African Americans into careers that for them were
non-traditional (and usually inaccessible). Although an unlikely
vehicle, Clark College became the means to help him advance his
vision.

Aside from its traditional liberal arts course offerings (which did
include a solid social sciences division), Clark had only two intro-

ductory courses in print journalism and a few science courses that might help prepare students for careers in medical technology. In conversation with several of us, he began to shape an image of three major additions to the Clark curriculum. "Who says we can't define the liberal arts the way we want?" he asked rhetorically. A flurry of foundation grants supported a mass communications center, an allied health curriculum, and the Southern Center for Studies in Public Policy began to take shape. Directed by Robert Kronley, the latter was the only undergraduate policy studies center in the country. Vivian also forged alliances with the Washington Research Project, a pioneering public interest law firm.[29] That connection enabled students to take advantage of summer internships and significant research opportunities that later led them into distinguished careers in academia, law, and government service.

One of my most gratifying memories of that period is from the afternoon I completed an application to the Federal Communications Commission for the license of what eventually would become WCLK-FM, now a well-known jazz radio station broadcasting from the campus. Another sense of achievement came years later when Spike Lee, the Academy Award-winning filmmaker, made it widely known that his career was first nurtured by Dr. Herbert Eichelberger, a faculty member of Clark's Mass Communications Center.

Even as we reconstructed the curriculum, Vivian was strengthening the board of trustees. He had inherited a well-meaning but not especially effectual group of white United Methodist bishop appointees and elderly Clark alumni, but quickly bolstered its ranks with figures like Vernon E. Jordan, Jr., CEO of the United Negro College Fund and later the National Urban League; Charles Kindleberger, an economist from the Massachusetts Institute of Technology; Philip Hammer, an architect and city planner; Louis Regenstein, a partner from a prominent Atlanta law firm, local architect Cecil Alexander, and some younger Clark alumni who were achieving professional

---

29 Founded by Marian Wright Edelman, Ruby Martin, and other prominent attorneys, it later would evolve into the Children's Defense Fund.

recognition. Before the recruitment process ended, the board included the CEO of Sears, Roebuck and Company and other national figures.

While shoring up the governance function, he especially reveled in the assembling of a multi-racial and multi-cultural faculty whose members enjoyed debate and programmatic experimentation. Vivian's interest in encouraging different points of view further manifested itself in the selection of speakers for student assemblies and college commencement exercises. And even though he was sensitive to student demands for Black identity, he pushed back against the separatist movement that was gaining strength on many of the HBCU campuses.

Fundraising for many Black colleges had been typified by college presidents going on the road with their student choirs, presenting concerts in Black and white churches, and asking for charitable offerings. We instead packaged our three new academic ventures into a fundraising campaign titled "Increasing the Options." The campaign was to be launched with a three-day series of seminars and a Black-tie kickoff banquet at the Waldorf Astoria Hotel in New York City.

Plans for the banquet were proceeding well. Vernon Jordan, one of Vivian's closest friends, had agreed to serve as the master of ceremonies, and we had arranged the requisite elaborate program demanded by this kind of occasion. It included greetings from the heads of prominent organizations, a keynote address by Morris Abram, the renowned Georgia civil rights lawyer who had been President of Brandeis University and Chair of the United Negro College Fund, and remarks by Vivian himself.

Pleased with what we had assembled, I called Vernon to share an outline of the program with him. After I finished, there was a long pause. Then Vernon's deep voice growled, "Brother Lehfeldt, when's da n*****s gonna sing?" He then delivered his succinct analysis of the planned occasion. If we were going to assemble an audience that included many wealthy white people to make the pitch for a Black college, history and tradition demanded that they be serenaded by a choir of African American voices. The sheer matter-of-factness of his insistence upon what I thought was an obsolete tradition caught me completely off guard. "Check with Vivian," he concluded.

Vivian listened carefully to my report and then laughed boisterously. "Damn," he finally declared. "He's right. I should have thought of it." He reached for the phone to call Dr. Florence Robinson, the head of the music department. Pragmatism carried the day.

The night of the Waldorf banquet, a student ensemble (with only a few ringers from the alumni ranks who had become professional singers) received standing applause after they performed selections from *Porgy and Bess* and familiar Negro spirituals.

The Chronicle of Higher Education put the Clark story on its front page with a picture of Vivian Henderson, looking very un-presidential in shirtsleeves, seated behind his desk with a big cigar and an even bigger grin.

One of the most exciting features of the fundraising campaign was the acceptance by Clark's formerly moribund alumni association of a seemingly impossible $500,000 goal that it met successfully. This achievement was due in no small measure to the dynamic leadership of alumna Juanita Eber, the college's new Director of Alumni Affairs.

For seven years Vivian and I worked hard and played hard together. It was one of the most productive and informative periods of my professional life. We turned out to be an effective development team as we traveled around the country to tell the Clark College story to prospective grant makers. Asked for my whereabouts one day, my wife responded, "Butch and Sundance are somewhere off robbing trains again." And without apology for a lack of humility, I will observe that we raised a lot of money.

Vivian became the first African American board member of The Ford Foundation, co-chairman of Mayor Maynard Jackson's Reorganization Task Force, and education co-chairman of then-Governor Jimmy Carter's Goals for Georgia Progress. Still other honors and responsibilities that recognized his intellect, imagination, and pioneering studies as an economist followed.

For all his gregarious good humor, Vivian could be tough. A major oil company discovered a privately owned lot on the corner of the Clark College campus and let it be known that it planned to purchase the property and put a filling station there. Vivian didn't bother with legal niceties. He simply confronted the corporate leadership and threatened to throw such a powerful, twenty-four-hour boycott around the establishment that it would never sell a drop of gas. Today that corner is the site of an attractive student center.

He could be outrageous. Preparing to begin his address to an academic leadership group that had never met him, he assured his audience that his presentation would be brief because he badly needed to relieve himself.

He could be witty. A white freshman had managed to enroll at Clark with the intention of playing on the football team but without discovering that he was coming to a historically Black college. He stayed and played, and when Vivian told the story, he always concluded with, "Now we're looking for one of them who can sing and one who can dance."

He could be ironic. Vivian, Robert Kronley, and I had just left The Temple, a synagogue in Atlanta, after a funeral service held for Alan Bussel, a young journalism professor who had died unexpectedly and of whom Vivian had been very fond. Still dealing emotionally with the loss, he declared, "I need a drink," and lead the way across Peachtree Street toward a small hotel on the other side. Marching on the sidewalk in front of the establishment was a picket line—a barrier he normally would have respected. He paused and considered the situation before stating, "Damn it, I still need a drink." In a plea to the famed Black trade unionist, he looked skyward and murmured, "Forgive me, Mr. Randolph,"[30] crossed the picket line, and proceeded to the bar.

He could be wry. Vivian wriggled around the tradition that honorary degrees could be presented only during spring commencement

---

30 A. Philip Randolph, founder of the Brotherhood of Sleeping Car Porters, and civil rights activist.

exercises and arranged for Duke Ellington to receive one during a winter event. A concert by the excellent Clark College Jazz Orchestra under the direction of James Patterson was wrapped around the degree presentation. One of the highlights of the evening occurred when Ellington sat down at the piano and joined the ensemble in a performance of "Take the 'A' Train." During a party for Ellington held at the president's residence later that evening, Vivian quipped, "Years from now, I guarantee you that everyone in the orchestra will be bragging about those days when they jammed with the Duke."

Vivian loved a good party whether he was the host or a guest and took special pride in the eggnog he personally concocted for his annual New Year's Day open house, to which the entire college family was invited.

And he could also be downright ornery. There was that evening when he and I had gone to Gallagher's, the famed steakhouse in Midtown Manhattan, across the street from the location of the original Madison Square Garden. The restaurant's walls were covered with framed photographs of prominent sports celebrities from the past. As we sipped our digestifs, Vivian fell silent while his gaze focused on those pictures. "There's not a single damn colored person on that wall," he declared. Rising to his feet and calling one of the waiters to his side, he marched toward the nearest wall that included famous white boxers. Pointing with a cane he was then using, he loudly demanded, "Where's Sugar Ray Robinson? Where's Archie Moore? Where's Jack Johnson?" People around the restaurant were taking notice, and a manger was approaching, but Vivian continued his circuit of the room. Arriving at a collection of photos of white basketball greats, he yelled "Where's Wilt Chamberlain? Where's Bill Russell? Where's Oscar Robertson?" When he finally located a picture of Jackie Robinson at the back of the room, he snorted with disgust. "This is pathetic. That's the best you can do?" Several of the patrons gave him a round of applause. As we finally took our leave and stepped outside, he grinned and said, "I think I got their attention."

Finally, despite his boisterous nature, he was humble. He delayed his inauguration and its corresponding expense at Clark for three years until he was satisfied that the college was again financially solvent. Unlike many other academic leaders, he found a way to utilize all of his important national contacts in ways that served to advance the college rather than simply redound to his personal benefit.

On the evening after Vivian died from a ruptured aneurysm on an operating table at Piedmont Hospital, I went home, drank a lot of bourbon, and cried uncontrollably for the better part of an hour over the loss of a father figure, brother, mentor, and friend. I didn't honor my own father with that much booze or that many tears.

Had he not passed away at the age of fifty-two, I have full confidence that Vivian W. Henderson would have gone on to become the president of a major foundation, a U.S. cabinet officer (he and Jimmy Carter knew each other), the occupant of an endowed professorship at a prestigious historically white university—perhaps all the above.

In later years, the financial difficulties of Atlanta University led it to seek a merger with Clark College. I contend that Clark was ready to assume that leadership role because of the risk-taking, initiative-seizing style of operation first introduced by Vivian Henderson.

Martin Lives in the 'Hood

Not too many years ago, we arranged a dinner party for a group of professional colleagues and their spouses who had gathered from around the country for a meeting in Atlanta. As we came to learn, a racially mixed carload of them was on the way to our home. Taking note of the fact that he was seeing an increasing number of Black faces as the car moved deeper into Southwest Atlanta, one of the African American passengers reportedly exclaimed with a mixture of surprise and delight, "Damn, Martin lives in the 'hood."

If they haven't been advised in advance about our residence in a predominantly Black neighborhood, that discovery can be a bit of a shock for some white visitors. Even if they have already been informed of that fact, they are likely to imagine that we are in a low-income area of frame bungalows in need of painting, or perhaps in a cluster of brick tenement buildings. No one seems to be prepared for a 4,000+ square foot dwelling situated on a hillside with nearly an acre of land and shaded by magnificent old oak trees. It would be extremely misleading to characterize our setting as a ghetto. How we got there may be worth a bit of explanation.

As I've already noted, my marital situation was in transition in the early 1970s—a situation that occupied much of my attention. Consequently, I was not paying especially close attention to other matters. I was obliquely aware that I was seeing more African Americans in our general area, but the extent of the shift in housing patterns was slow to dawn on me. Then one morning on my way to work, as I left our apartment complex and crossed Campbellton Road, I suddenly realized that every house in the next block of

Honeysuckle Lane had a FOR SALE sign in the front yard. Panic-stricken white folks, frightened by cynical, block-busting real estate agents—both white and Black—were fleeing my part of town in droves. (Included in the escaping horde were white members of the allegedly progressive church that I had started to attend.)

This frenetic activity happened to coincide with my own interest in buying a home. I planned to be at Clark College for at least several more years, and I suspected that the job would continue to entail travel. A good location for a residence would be within easy reach of both the campus and the airport. My new wife, Ann, and I were attracted to the Adams Park neighborhood. It was a heavily wooded part of the city with older homes that included many handsome bungalows as well as larger structures in a wide variety of architectural designs. Our search began.

As we came to learn, that part of the city had been a kind of blue-collar—although also thoroughly white—version of Buckhead. (Buckhead was the home of the city's leading corporate executives, attorneys, and physicians.) Many of Southwest Atlanta's largest homes belonged to white families who owned their own successful businesses. They were well off financially but probably did not belong to the elite Capital City Club or Piedmont Driving Club.

I naïvely assumed that the housing shuffle I have described would soon subside. As if to confirm my optimism, a neighborhood organization named SWAP (Southwest Atlantans for Progress), a bi-racial coalition of homeowners, was on record as being committed to establishing a racially integrated part of the city.

We kept looking.

One chilly, early winter evening, our white real estate agent, who lived in the Adams Park section, ushered us from a driveway up the outdoor steps to the front door and first floor of a large white brick home. We stepped into a spacious, sunken living room with exposed beams. The flames from the oak logs burning in the fireplace threw off both light and heat. The setting exuded warmth and welcome.

Still standing on the landing by the front door, I blurted out,

"We'll take it," effectively destroying any bargaining position I might have had. Cost, however, turned out not to be a major factor in the negotiations. One of the bonuses of the racial transitioning that was going on was the drop in asking prices. Many white folks were so desperate to sell and escape the likelihood of acquiring Black neighbors that they were willing to take significant financial losses.

To shorten the story, we did indeed purchase the charm-exuding property. The original structure, built in 1935, was reportedly modeled after the owner's favorite cottage in Scotland. Subsequent residents had constructed additions, and we would eventually continue that tradition. The house had four bedrooms and three baths, as well as a living room, dining room, and enormous den. The asking price, although reasonable, was more than I could afford. (The down payment itself was more than I could afford, given the less-than-princely salary that Clark was paying me.) But I scratched together the deposit with help from my mother and some trusting friends, and we made the move.

Home ownership was a heady experience for a preacher's kid who had never lived in anything except a parsonage, a dormitory, or an apartment. I was a stranger to the world of property maintenance and the tools required to preserve one's home and land in reasonably civilized shape—assuming that one knew how to use all of those tools in the first place.

It's neither here nor there, but over the years I have paid a steady stream of both professional contractors and so-called handymen of varying ability to keep our aging property in reasonably good shape. As an older man with degrees in English literature and theology, I am in no position to offer anything other than moral support to the work of renovation. I bow in abject awe to anyone who can examine a leaky roof (or leaky anything), diagnose the problem, and fix it.

Because it still rankles me, I need to share one last story about our relocation. The people from whom we bought our new home were a "Christian" couple whose "ministry" was caring for the children of missionaries serving elsewhere in the world. The house they showed us looked well cared for and freshly painted. However, on the day we arrived and began hauling our belongings from the moving van into the house, we discovered that the fresh paint had been selectively applied. Thus, for example, in the master bedroom, the space on the wall that had been hidden by the headboard still had the earlier coat of paint on it. Another goodbye present from those God-fearing scam artists was their wrapping of the cowling on the dishwasher motor with wads of paper towels to hide a bad leak—something that didn't become evident until after a week of its use. The list continues . . . but I've made my point.

Even as I was concluding my purchase of the big house on the hill, most of the remaining white people in the neighborhood, including those stalwart members of the ironically named SWAP, were selling their homes to new African American residents and moving to the other side of town. Within short order, we were an almost exclusively Black neighborhood.

White people meeting us and learning where we lived often would ask with concern, "How long do you think you'll be able to stay there?" They appeared genuinely confused when we explained that we had just moved in and planned to remain. A few of them had grown up and gone to school in the area before joining the early evacuees. Others who had lived elsewhere in Atlanta their entire lives didn't have a clue where our neighborhood was located.

What I've been describing was going on all over the New South. To be sure, the wealthy residents of the region's most prestigious zip codes (places like Buckhead in Atlanta; Nashville's Belle Meade; Charlotte's Myers Park; Windsor Farms in Richmond; and Mountain View in Birmingham) could dig in and hold the line. Few African Americans could then afford to move into those neighborhoods. Elsewhere, though, the musical chairs game of middle-class real estate transaction was moving at a gallop.

Change eventually came, but there were at first downsides to being in a newly African American enclave. *The New York Times* wouldn't deliver to our zip code, even though our neighbors like Andrew Young and John Lewis, who lived half a mile away, and other prominent public figures, were often front-page copy in that same newspaper. Shopping, too, could be a challenge. A lot of stores were slow to discover what economic studies had been showing for years: the Black middle and upper classes had great purchasing power. We would encounter our neighbors at "good" grocery stores on the other side of town.

On the other hand, we were easily recognizable and no one on our side of town asked Ann for identification when she paid for goods or services with a check. On another occasion, as we were planning a large party, the public works department had steadfastly ignored our request to repair a pothole on the street in front of our house. A call to City Hall with the information that Mayor Shirley Franklin, another neighbor, was on the guest list had a crew on the job within a couple of hours.

For several years, when driving around our part of town, my wife and I were prone to holler, "There's one!" when we spotted a white person in the vicinity. Presumably, Black residents expressed similar surprise when someone white who was not a delivery person, a meter reader, a census taker, or a member of our family made an appearance in our neck of the woods.

Those days are now long gone. Thanks to the efforts of Marvin Arrington, former City Council President and Superior Court judge, who used to live near us, and other African American movers and shakers, we now are within minutes of two supermarkets, a Home Depot, a Wal-Mart, Starbucks, a plethora of gas stations, a popular Asian fusion restaurant, and a host of fast-food franchises.

After nearly half a century, our neighborhood is also now experiencing a new kind of change in its residential makeup. It began about a decade ago. One of our few white neighbors, with whom we often joked about our minority status, was one of the first people to spot the "trend." He pounded on our kitchen door one morning. When I let him in, Bill waved a newspaper article in my face. "Look," he said. "We're no longer a 97% Black neighborhood; now it's only 96%."

Atlanta has been witnessing a surge in urban population. The children of white people who fled to the suburbs in the 1960s are discovering the joys of urban life and daily routines that don't include commuting, mowing the lawn, or worrying about the condition of septic tanks. The grandchildren of Black people who escaped the once-dominant racism of the region are returning and going to work for the major companies that too are returning to the downtown areas. With increased residential density comes the construction of new apartment houses and condominiums and the renovation of long-forsaken industrial properties like factories, mills, and warehouses. Popping up to serve these new urbanites are new restaurants, coffeehouses, cleaners, shops, and markets. Sections of the city that once were abandoned after the sun set are now centers of night life.

Even with rapid-paced construction, this new residential pattern has pushed the cost of both purchased and rental property beyond the reach of many would-be urban dwellers. Seeking the next best option, this new crop of young white and Black professionals has looked beyond the core city and discovered old and often forgotten close-in neighborhoods, both white and Black, that had fallen on hard times. There they quickly discover that it is possible to purchase these residences in need of repair and to restore them for far less than the cost of a downtown condo or loft.

Yet even those opportunities have not slaked the hunger of young singles and couples who want to be close to the urban action. They now look a bit farther out from the center of the city and discover neighborhoods that were the original "suburbs"—in the days when streetcars enabled folks to move beyond the increasingly crowded downtowns. The developers of these communities at times included amenities like small lakes, terraced terrains, and small parks.

Adams Park, where we live, has some of those features and a public golf course and public swimming pool, too. And so, as I noted, our middle-class community, made especially attractive by heavily wooded and large lots, is being rediscovered. We and other neighborhoods on our side of town that fifty years ago became almost totally African American are slowly taking on a paler complexion again. Increasingly, as we drive through the neighborhood, we see white couples walking their dogs, white parents pushing baby carriages, and white joggers.

An angry young African American activist at a neighborhood meeting I attended railed against the change that is underway. The first clues that white folks are starting to move in, he predicted, are the arrival of coffeehouses and then bike lanes painted on the streets.

However, his racial bias is misdirected; gentrification is a matter of class and economics, not just color. Middle-class African Americans also are settling in the neighborhood, and they too ride bicycles and jog and hang out in shops that sell over-priced coffee and wine. Within months of the gathering I mentioned, a Black-owned coffeehouse opened next door to the place we were meeting. A parallel development has been the construction of obscenely large McMansions in gated Black communities into which the residents drive in their BMWs, Mercedes, and low-slung Italian sports cars.

It is my sense that our neighborhood will, during the coming years, comfortably settle into being a "salt-and-pepper," but still predominantly African American, middle-class community. It probably won't happen in my lifetime, but I feel safe in further forecasting that eventually the elementary school across the street will be racially integrated and of a quality that will attract everyone's children. In Adams Park, at least, perhaps yet another New South will come into being.

School Days

A ll too soon after our move to Adams Park, it was time to decide where our children would be educated. To put it more baldly, were the kids going to go to public or private school? We were able to delay the decision for a while because Georgia still had not introduced statewide pre-school or kindergarten education. Liz and Conrad went to an excellent Montessori school in the neighborhood with a few other white children and the offspring of Black celebrities like Maynard Jackson; Freddy Cole (the jazz-singing brother of Nat "King" Cole); Dr. Hamilton Holmes (who with Charlayne Hunter had integrated the University of Georgia); and professors from the Atlanta University Center.

My parents' financial sacrifices had enabled me to gain the benefits of an excellent private school education, and I carried an initial bias against the quality of the Atlanta school system. However, my new wife had attended public schools (albeit in the Upper Peninsula of Michigan) and she was opposed to the idea that we should increase our poverty level for the sake of the children. After a great deal of debate, we enrolled them as the only white kids in the neighborhood elementary schools for a year or so. It was no more a good idea than sending a single Black child to an all-white school to achieve racial integration. Then, taking advantage of a loophole in a convoluted, court-approved desegregation system, for the rest of their Atlanta school years until graduation, they went on to attend the few racially balanced public schools on the other side of town.

They received a better-than-average education—good enough to earn them generous college scholarships and thereby keep their non-profitable father from deeper insolvency. Liz was her class vale-dictorian; Conrad earned salutatorian status and became a Cadet Lieutenant Colonel and Battalion Commander of the Northside High School ROTC unit.

Perhaps they gained something else too. At one point, Liz got romantically involved for a while with a young African American guy in her class, who arranged to escort her to the junior prom. When he expressed nervousness about what her father's reaction might be to his attentions, she was able to laugh and tell him, "That's probably the last thing you need to worry about."

Both Liz and Conrad became "multilingual"—able to converse in the English we spoke at home, to mimic the drawl of Ann's parents and other native white Southerners, and to be comfortable with what in those days was referred to as ebonics.

Conrad was a substitute (the sole "white shadow") on the high school basketball team. Driving him home from practice one evening, I happened to mention that we had once considered sending him and his sister to a private school whose name I shared. His disbelief approached outrage. "That's not the real world, Dad," he protested.

There remain a few public schools in metro Atlanta that are racially integrated, but most of the rest are nearly all-Black or all-white. As is the case throughout the South (and indeed the nation), the quality of the education they offer is heavily dependent upon the economic strength of the neighborhoods they serve.

Both Black and white families who can pay the expensive freight send their children to the hundreds of private preparatory schools scattered throughout the region. Some of these institutions have long and distinguished histories; others began as segregated academies, called into being as a defiant response to *Brown v. Board. of Education* in 1954. Most of them maintained all-white enrollments until many years later, and even today some are only "tokenly" integrated. There also are broadly Christian and Jewish and expressly denominational institutions, whose theological stances range from progressive to appallingly conservative. Some are truly excellent; then again, some of the others constitute a respectable and reasonably satisfactory way to make sure your children don't have to be placed in contact with too many kids of other races, ethnic backgrounds, religions, or lower economic classes.

The overall picture of public-school education throughout the region is not promising. Several of the states still do not have widespread public pre-school or kindergarten programming and, for the most part, public schools are woefully under-budgeted. No matter which criteria are used to measure achievement (teacher quality, dropout rates, SAT scores), the elementary, middle, and high schools of the Southern states, especially in the Deep South, often anchor the bottom of the scales. I can cite as many exceptions to my generalizations as anyone else, but I remain convinced that this state of affairs continues to be one of the most disheartening features of life in the region and the one most likely to retard the development of the South.

History Lessons

Lift ev'ry voice and sing,
Till earth and heaven ring,
Ring with the harmonies of liberty . . .

Fifty years ago, it would have been nearly impossible to assemble a roomful of white folks anywhere who knew the words I have just posted or who could sing the music that accompanied them.

Memorizing that text and melody was just one of the many expansions of my knowledge that accompanied the move to Clark College. Years earlier—perhaps in a book by James Baldwin—I had seen mention of the "Negro National Anthem,"[31] but I didn't have a clue about the meaning of that reference. Within short order, though, I came to know all three verses of this powerful choral celebration. (Today, it appears in the hymnals of historically white church denominations and is taught to public school students, thereby enriching many more lives.)

My new life was filled with other discoveries. I remember with

---

31 James Weldon Johnson (1871-1938) wrote "Lift Ev'ry Voice and Sing" as a poem that was then set to music by his brother, John Rosamond Johnson, in 1899. It was first publicly performed in the Johnsons' hometown of Jacksonville, Florida, by five hundred schoolchildren at the segregated Stanton School, where the author was then principal, to celebrate Abraham Lincoln's birthday in 1900. James Weldon Johnson later joined the staff of the National Association for the Advancement of Colored People (NAACP) and became that organization's executive secretary in 1920. (The NAACP also adopted the Johnson brothers' work as its official anthem.) Johnson's distinguished career includes being a leading figure in the Harlem Renaissance, being appointed by President Theodore Roosevelt as U.S. Consul in Venezuela and Nicaragua, becoming the first African American professor at New York University, and later joining the faculty of Fisk University.

special pleasure being educated about the meaning of a mysterious (to me) event on the calendar that folks called Juneteenth.[32] Thanks to a highly publicized, ill-advised, loudly protested, and subsequently cancelled plan to hold a political rally for President Trump on June 19, 2020, millions of white Americans learned why that date is special to Black Americans.

The proposed rally, postponed until the next day, took place in Tulsa—a city well known to African Americans as the site of one of the most vicious examples of white mob violence against Black people in the history of the United States. It may have topped the charts for cruelty, but as I soon learned, the country's history was filled with examples of similar brutality. Perhaps the most important lesson was that anything labeled by white folks as a "race riot" (like the Atlanta conflict in 1906) likely as not was an unprovoked attack by white people upon African Americans.[33]

Another revered Black tradition that was new to me was Watch Night. Many Christian churches have long-standing traditions of holding services on New Year's Eve to reflect on the past year, confess faults and misdeeds, and pray for strength to do better in the coming year. According to African American tradition, on December 31, 1862, it took on new meaning. Word had reached many slaves that an emancipation proclamation signed by President Lincoln would go into effect the next day. They gathered in their churches and dwelling places to await the confirmation of that news. Today, many African American congregations come together on the last day of the year for services that may include singing, dancing, and a haunting call-and-response countdown to midnight.

---

32 Juneteenth is the oldest nationally celebrated commemoration of the ending of slavery in the United States. On June 19, 1865, more than two years after Abraham Lincoln signed the Emancipation Proclamation and two months after General Robert E. Lee surrendered to General Ulysses S. Grant in Virginia, Union troops informed thousands of African Americans in Galveston, Texas, that all slaves in the Confederate states had been freed.

33 Among those white massacres of African Americans that failed to make it into the history books until recently were those in Memphis (1866), Camilla, GA and Opelousas, LA (1868), Meridian, MS (1871), Clinton, MS (1875) . . . the list goes on.

To repeat an earlier point: my move to Atlanta and Clark College did not deposit me in an African American slum. My residential and occupational immersion was into a Black middle-class and upper-class world—a section of American society that I previously had no idea existed.

It was a world whose inhabitants used the infamous "Green Book"[34] to guide their travels through the deeply segregated "hospitality" industry. It also was a world of fraternities, sororities, social clubs, professional societies, and other parallels to the one inhabited by middle- and upper-class whites. There were even separate recreation destinations like the seaside resorts of Highland Beach in Maryland, established by Frederick Douglass's son; American Beach on Amelia Island in Florida; Atlantic Beach, tucked between Myrtle Beach and North Myrtle Beach in South Carolina; and, for those who could afford it, the Oak Bluffs section of Martha's Vineyard off the coast of Massachusetts.

This world included Jack and Jill,[35] the national membership organization with hundreds of chapters wherein young mothers could both shield their offspring from cruel discrimination and provide them with the kinds of positive cultural, social, and recreational experiences from which they would otherwise have been banned. Those children learned to perform classical music on the piano and stringed instruments; they visited museums; some of them learned to swim and even ski.

Although many Black college students whom I met were the first in their families to attend college, many others were simply the latest in a long line of relatives for whom higher education was a routine experience.

---

34 As portrayed in a recent Hollywood production that received mixed reviews in the Black community, the Green Book (actual name: *The Negro Motorist Green Book*) was first produced in 1936 by a Black postal worker named Victor Hugo Green, to direct African Americans to restaurants and hotels where they would be welcomed and not encounter overt discrimination or threats of violence.

35 Founded in Philadelphia in 1938, Jack and Jill of America, Inc. continues to be a strong national organization that promotes youth leadership, volunteer service, financial literacy, civic involvement, and legislative advocacy.

Who knew about this remarkable record of self-protection and achievement against great odds? Who would have guessed? It was all a big secret from me and most of my white "cousins." The "discovery" of an African American middle- and upper-class violated all the white stereotypes. In doing so, it also made it much more difficult for whites to spout thoughtless cliches or listen to broad and usually uninformed generalizations about African Americans.

A Rite of Passage

One of the more significant events to mark my passage toward Southern citizenship occurred on May 30, 1977. It was the day we staged the First Annual Memorial Day Pig Roast at our home. Memories of that jamboree have since become the stuff of legend.

Our decision to roast a pig was rooted in sheer fantasy. We had no idea what we were doing, but we pushed ahead. Lip-smacking friends with memories of past pig-pickin's offered lots of advice through which we sorted as our plan took shape.

A neighbor volunteered to dig a pit on the hill behind our house. By the time he finished, its surface dimensions were larger than a grave, but not as deep. (To this day, the filled-in but still sunken site looks as if it belongs in a Civil War cemetery.)

My mother-in-law found a knowledgeable veteran of many pig roasts out in Oconee County. She commissioned him to weld together a magnificent "stretcher." That's the device that enables one to hold the pig in place over the heat source, flip it during the cooking process, and remove it when it is cooked. The sturdy one he produced was formed from rebar rods and strong baling wire.

Using a long-since forgotten formula, we determined that we would need an animal that weighed about 150-200 pounds. A couple of days before the celebration, Ann and the aptly named Steve Bacon, our church's associate pastor, headed to the old State Farmer's Market south of town and purchased a large porker. They weren't prepared for a question from the vendor about whether they wanted to keep the animal's head. After a quick conference, though, they voted for decapitation. They drove from the market to our down-town church and wrestled the headless hog into the kitchen's walk-in refrigerator. There it would remain until the evening before the celebration.

Even as these preparations for the main course of the Memorial Day meal were underway, we were organizing the rest of the feast. We had very limited financial resources in those days. Consequently, we charged an attendance fee to the two hundred invited guests and further assigned them the tasks of preparing and/or bringing baked beans, coleslaw, other salads, iced tea, lemonade, and beer, as well as pies and other desserts.

The evening before the holiday we filled the pit with split wood, set it ablaze, and watched until the flames turned to glowing coals. It was then time to fasten the pig into its stretcher, rest each end of the stretcher on cinder blocks, and begin the cooking process. For the next fifteen-plus hours, shifts of volunteers added wood to the fire, drank beer, and regularly flipped the pig. The marvelous aroma of pork fat dripping into the hot pit wafted through the night air. Bill, the pit-digger, stretched a long extension cord from our house to a black and white television set, so those on duty could enjoy a bit of late-night viewing. (Ted Turner had not yet launched CNN, so program fare following the eleven o'clock news consisted primarily of travelogues and test patterns on the limited number of channels.)

The pig continued to cook through the morning hours, while Ann tended a cast iron pot of Brunswick stew. I had found a James Beard recipe for this delicacy that began, "Skin four squirrels." Ignoring that instruction, we elected to use only chicken and pork. We were guided by the wisdom of another Oconee County farmer who had tersely advised me, "Whatever the hell you do, don't put any beef in it. If you do, it'll look like something the dog throwed up."

By noon, the guests were beginning to arrive, and the bounte-ous feast was being arranged on the patio beside the house. A profes-sor from Columbia Seminary brought his violin to provide musical accompaniment. It seemed only fitting to encourage him to scramble up a ladder and serenade us from the roof of the back porch. At the appointed hour (after much debate over whether the meat was ready), the pig was lifted onto a large makeshift table constructed from a sheet of plywood and sawhorses. A pathologist friend from Emory University elected himself head of the surgical team to dismember our roasted swine. As John noted, he hadn't had the chance to wield a scalpel since medical school. (If I remember correctly, he brought his own.) Soon the crowd was devouring mounds of tender meat and "cracklin's" with all the fixin's.

A volleyball tournament after the feast was interrupted by a torrential deluge that left most of the players covered with mud. I lined them up and hosed them down like prisoners at the county jail, but the interior of the house never completely recovered from people tramping dirt and debris through the place for the rest of the afternoon. Meanwhile, "Granny" Kimes, down from Tennessee for a visit with her family, commandeered the upright piano and began belting out old gospel hymns and popular tunes from the past.

Postscript: Because it was beastly hot on the First Annual Memorial Day Pig Roast, we scheduled the second annual event for the next September. It, too, was a great success. Our friend, Betty Talmadge, the wife of Georgia's senior senator, attended. She had just co-authored *How to Cook a Pig*,[36] but watched everything with keen interest from her perch on the back porch swing. As she confessed. she herself had never attempted what we accomplished.

One of these days, we really need to get around to scheduling the Third Annual Memorial Day Pig Roast. That "stretcher" I described is still in the basement.

---

36 Betty Talmadge and Jean Robitscher, *How to Cook a Pig and Other Back-to-the-Farm Recipes* (New York: Simon and Schuster, 1977).

My Sense of Place

One of the highest compliments I ever received came after I had lived in the region long enough to establish a few credentials. Bob Hull introduced me to a Southern audience as a fellow Southerner, graciously noting it wasn't my fault that my mother had given birth to me in New York City.

I still am flattered whenever (and it *has* been known to happen) people identify me as being from "here." But to be honest, what does that mean these days? Contrary to the opinion of a few diehards, one need not have an ancestor who wore a Confederate uniform or owned a big white house with columns on the front porch to qualify for that distinction. It's also not necessary to be the descendant of slaves or sharecroppers.

Somewhere in the mountains of eastern Tennessee is a white, toothless auto mechanic with a Confederate flag decal in the rear window of his pick-up truck who, for all I know, handles snakes in church on Sunday. That stereotypical figure certainly considers himself to be a Southerner.

Another Southerner is an elegant Black Harvard Law graduate in his art-filled, Buckhead condo overlooking Peachtree Street, who is a partner in one of the city's most prestigious legal firms. So too is the underpaid elementary school principal in the Black Belt of Alabama, with educational, cultural, and religious values and achievements that place her squarely in the middle class. Still other Southerners are the clusters of homeless people on the region's city streets whose continued presence defies the best intentions of the good people who want to help them.

Southerners come in all hues and levels of economic status and mental health. Their educational backgrounds differ widely, and they have a variety of shapes, sizes, and dental conditions. For a growing number, English is not their native tongue. In short, increasingly they defy generalization.

I know fellow Southerners who like to invoke their "sense of place." The phrase denotes a mystically blended, reverential "memory" of sight, sound, touch, taste, and smell that captures the essence of where they were born and raised. Usually, but not always, these localities are small, mainly homogenous communities, often in a rural setting. (It is my observation that one usually does not derive this magical, near-religious sense of place from life on the eighteenth floor of an urban condominium or in a suburban tract home.)

By the way, identifying a sense of place can lapse into rank boosterism. I still recall the morning that I received a telephone call from a fellow in Alabama. He wanted to explore how he and his colleagues might begin the formation of a community foundation. Before listening to my recommendations, though, he launched into a serenade to his town that was worthy of a Chamber of Commerce executive. Winding down finally, he concluded, "And I'll have you know that we are the third-largest city south of Montgomery." I guess we all need to lay claim to uniqueness—our very own sense of place.

There are nostalgic observers who go so far as to describe the current version of the region as the "No South"—devoid of all the positive and humanizing features that once undergirded its sense of place. Although not a purebred Southerner, I disagree. Charming and endearing characteristics still abound.

My connection with the South is like a second marriage. I walked into it with reasonably open eyes—certainly not blind to the faults of my new partner but also not inclined to try to correct them with frontal attacks. Instead, in my own way, I have tried to offer alternatives to those patterns of thinking and behavior that I found off-putting. The hallmarks of my feelings about the union have been deep care, recognition of ways in which my new partner compensates for my failings, and genuine delight in the quirky differences that can be unsettling without damaging our relationship.

Go Dawgs!³⁷

The second family into which I married was very Southern. How Southern? Well, when the birth of his daughter (she whom I would eventually marry) drew near, my father-in-law-to-be moved his wife from Illinois to Hannibal, Missouri[38] so their little girl could never be identified as a Yankee by virtue of birth.

He also had played football for the University of Georgia. One of the family's sacred relics was a clipping of a column by Ralph McGill (then simply a sportswriter, not yet known as the "conscience of the South") devoted to my father-in-law's gridiron exploits. In later life, he always had season tickets on the fifty-yard line for home games, so it was inevitable that I would eventually be invited to attend one of them.

To understand my experience fully, it's important to keep in mind that I graduated from a small, all-male, liberal arts undergraduate institution in the Northeast. (Southern Presbyterians may picture a Yankee version of Davidson College before it went co-ed.) If he was lucky, our coach might be able to get eighteen players suited up for a Saturday football game against another Division III team—which then would usually trounce us. If we scored at all, the number of points was a multiple of six because we had no one on the team who could kick the ball between the goal posts after a touchdown for the extra point.

---

37 Adapted from Martin Lehfeldt, "Welcome South, Brother," a guest column for "Jamil's Georgia" in the Saporta Report, December 8, 2014.

38 For further clarification, google the Missouri Compromise of 1820 to discover why some considered that state to be "Southern."

On a pleasant autumn afternoon, there might be seventy or eighty people wearing jeans and sweaters lolling in the wooden bleachers on the home side of the field, some of them reading books. A well-worn story about our little college involved the first-time visitor who came to watch a football game on a Saturday afternoon. He parked his car and followed a crowd of people across the campus, only to discover they were headed to the library.

The visiting team usually brought a uniformed marching band, but we relied upon our casually garbed Drum and Kazoo Corps (exactly what it sounds like: one bass drum and perhaps twenty-five kazoos) to entertain the fans at halftime—and yes, we had a few marching maneuvers too.

It was a bright fall day when I arrived in Athens for my first Southeastern Conference match. I joined tens of thousands of rabid Georgia fans pushing and squeezing their way into Sanford Stadium. Many of the women wore dresses and heels. Several wore white gloves. I remember little about the game itself, except that the Bulldogs lost to the Kentucky Wildcats. However, I vividly recall that before the kickoff, Charles, the Prince of Wales, was introduced. (I still haven't a clue why he was there.) Much more exciting, James Brown, the Godfather of Soul, performed between the halves, and the almost totally white crowd screamed and shook hysterically. If I hadn't realized it before, I now was convinced that I had crossed over into a very different universe.

To be sure, within several years, we ex-Yankees were fanatically screaming "Go, Dawgs!" as Herschel (pronounced "Hushel" by my new family) Walker led the Georgia Bulldogs to a national championship and won the Heisman Trophy.

Joys of Southern Cooking

Further evidence of my acquired Southern citizenship is the change my taste buds have undergone.

- Although my Southern wife isn't fond of them, I have developed an appetite for greens—collards, turnip, whatever—with a liberal sprinkling of hot pepper sauce. Black-eyed peas and red beans and rice rank highly too.

- My family contends that I crossed the dietary fault line when I began helping myself to chitterlings, or "chitlin's" at Em McNair's New Year's Day party. It's the only time of year that I get to eat them, and only two of the Black guests and none of the other white folks at this event will go near them.

- I like grits, and I love cheese grits—a major shift for the fellow who used to sprinkle sugar on his Cream of Wheat.

- Two of my favorite main courses are fried catfish and barbeque.

- Because I am not a native, I don't feel fully qualified to engage in loud arguments about the relative merits of commercially prepared mayonnaise. For whatever interest it may hold, though, I read somewhere that Duke's Mayonnaise, first developed in Greenville, SC, during the Civil War, is the most popular among Southerners. Hellmann's, despite having been first concocted in New York City by an immigrant from Prussia, has many fans, and Blue Plate (created in Gretna, Louisiana) and Mrs. Filbert's (a product of Virginia) have their own advocates.

- How in the world did I survive for the better part of thirty years without discovering pimento cheese? It is a leading candidate for being named the true ambrosia of the South (as opposed to that infamous fruit and marshmallow concoction). My research has yet to produce a reliable answer about the origin of this delicacy. It doesn't matter. I'm just glad it exists and is widely available. I also am a firm believer that no reception after a funeral or memorial service is complete without the plentiful availability of pimento cheese sandwiches on white bread, sliced diagonally with the crusts cut off. (My instructions about arrangements for the reception after my own demise are very specific on this point.)

- A dear friend and former colleague grew up in South Georgia where her family's culinary rule of thumb was, "If it ain't fried, it ain't food." For health reasons, I don't follow that dictum, but all bets are off when it comes to crispy, non-greasy fried chicken.

- It probably could go without mention that I wash down all these taste treats with copious amounts of sweet tea.

Here are several other random pointers that I have formulated to guide my dietary routine:

- Don't undercook green beans. They don't have to be gray when they've finished cooking, but they shouldn't be crisp. (A tablespoon of bacon grease or a small chunk of fatback can do nothing except improve this dish.)

- Macaroni 'n' cheese is a vegetable—as confirmed by where it is listed on the menu in any authentically Southern eating establishment.

- Sugar does not belong on the list of ingredients for cornbread.

- Okra is delicious and does not have to be slimy.

- Fried green tomatoes may not have originated in the South

(One authority I read traces them back to the kitchens of Jewish immigrants from Europe.) Nonetheless, the South has perfected this dish.

- Buttermilk biscuits with breakfast are a wonderful way to start the day. I don't make them myself, but a good substitute can be found in a bag of Mary B's Frozen Biscuits (whose home base is Pensacola, Florida).

- Fine old recipes can be found in the cookbooks that Southern "women of the church" used to publish, but I recommend avoiding those that were popular during a period in history when marshmallows and Jell-O salads were in vogue.

I began learning to cook in the South. Whether I would have acquired this ability up north is questionable. When I lived up there, the whole enterprise, as I heard it being discussed by people who enjoyed cooking, sounded pretentious and off-putting. It invariably featured lengthy discussions about hard-to-find ingredients, specialized kitchen utensils, and the relative merits of different olive oils. (Sad to say, this highfalutin approach to the culinary arts has been finding its way into the conversation of the urban South.)

My venture into the world of food preparation began at the start of a summer vacation. Our funds were limited, so we decided to stay home and use the four weeks to become better acquainted with inexpensive amusements in the Atlanta area.

The second day of the new routine, I was sitting in my bathrobe, enjoying a second cup of coffee, and reading the *The Atlanta Constitution*. The sounds of children playing happily elsewhere in the house were a pleasant backdrop to the calm in the kitchen. Ann sat down beside me. As I recall, the conversation went something like this:

Ann: "Do I get a vacation too?"

Me: "What do you mean?"

Ann: "You're getting ready to stop going to work for a month."

Me (Cautiously) "Yes?"

Ann was a gourmet cook, who always seemed to enjoy herself in the kitchen, so I was caught off guard when she threw down this gauntlet: "Why don't you take over preparing dinners for the next month?" The challenge, frankly, was a bit intimidating, but I've always enjoyed betting on long shots. I accepted the dare.

The kids probably suffered the most during the early days of the new regime in the kitchen. During the first week, every single meal consisted of a variety of ground beef, pasta, and a tomato product. Things improved as I became more daring, although the night I produced a so-called "stone soup" that tasted like dishwater is still the stuff of family legend. By the third week, when I was asking Ann to pick up seldom-used spices and condiments at the supermarket, she added a codicil to our arrangement: if I were going to cook, I would have to create my offerings from food and drink already in the pantry.

She resumed kitchen duties after I returned to work, but I offered to cook Sunday dinners. In the process, I made a useful discovery. My previously not-always-approved-of routine of spending Sunday afternoons sipping bourbon and watching professional football suddenly became socially acceptable when the television set and the Makers' Mark were placed beside the kitchen stove. I even toyed with the notion of writing a cookbook for men who might benefit from this kind of multitasking arrangement.

A Language All Our Own

Distinctly Southern expressions are part of the background music that enhances life in the South. Some of them even have crept into my own vocabulary.

Recently I caught myself saying that I was *fixin' to get me* some collards at the store, and, while I was at it, that I *might could* look for some fatback. There was a time when I *reckon* (not suppose) that kind of sentence would have made me wince. Now I must concentrate hard to think of a better way to express the thought. *Gracious!*

I heard perhaps my all-time favorite Southernism during an evening meeting of a church leadership group. Our discussion had brought us to agreement about the wording of a new policy statement. Bob Bryan summarized our satisfaction by declaring, "*I b'lieve that dog'll hunt!*"

There are times when a statement like "that's wonderful" is simply not sufficient to convey appreciation for a treat like a slice of fresh-baked sweet potato pie. Bursting out with "*C'est magnifique!*" is only going to confuse folks, so in those cases, I have been known to rely upon "*Boy, howdy!*"

I have no idea what it means; it's a phrase I picked up in New Jersey from an American literature scholar with degrees from Harvard College, Union Theological Seminary, and Princeton University. However, having been raised in these parts and spent much of his career in Texas, Walter's speech has never lost its Southern cadence and texture (an interesting counterpoint to the East Tennessee twang and expressions of his wife, Margie). The phrase never fit naturally into my conversation when I lived in the North. In my current setting, though, it seems to be exactly the right way to voice excitement about almost anything.

Along the same line, there's another simple expression that both Linda and I now use regularly to express agreement or appreciation. It's one we picked up from Mike Calloway, our former AC repairman from Alabama. When, for example, Mike was working on the compressor, a typical conversation might go like this:

Me: Sure feels like it's gonna be a hot one today, Mike.

Mike: Shoot, yeah!

And so now around our household it would not be uncommon on a brisk fall day to hear me declare, "I'm guessin' it might be about time to head up to Elijay and buy us a basket of apples," and for Linda to respond, "Shoot, yeah!"

One of the first lessons that a Northerner who relocates to the South needs to learn is that "Gimme a little sugah" is not a request to pass the white, granular, sweet substance that sits in a little bowl in the middle of the table. It was at Clark College that I was educated to the understanding that I was being asked for a kiss. Also at Clark, I was introduced to the understanding that having significant wealth was best described as being "in high cotton."

The invitation "Y'all come see us" or "Y'all come back" should not necessarily be interpreted literally. Neither should the offer to be "carried" to church or a doctor appointment or the Piggly Wiggly.

If something is not a matter of particular concern, that indifference can well be described as "not givin' a lick," and a suitable description of an individual who is prone to imbibe too much is "He's bad to drink." Finally, an excellent way to convey the closeness with which one came to doing or feeling something after being shocked or startled is to use the expression "like to have," as in:

"When I heard she married her first cousin . . . I like to have died."

"When I learned I had won the lottery . . . I like to have fainted."

"When I saw that eighteen-wheeler barreling toward us in our lane . . . I like to have s***."

4WayBbq

We had been driving for several hours on a Sunday afternoon as we returned home from a short holiday on the Redneck Riviera. We were also beginning to pay the price for having chosen to follow back roads; what few restaurants we passed were closed.

Hunger pangs turned my thoughts to barbeque. Unlike many native Southerners, I do not get into arguments over the relative merits of chopped vs. pulled meat, or the tanginess of the sauce, or the sweetness of the beans, or the amount of vinegar in the slaw, or other elements of this unique branch of the culinary arts. I'm not wild about mustard-based sauce, preferring a tomato foundation, but I'll eat the former without a fuss if it's put before me. I certainly won't go to the mat, as one reviewer did, over the absence of lima beans in a Brunswick stew. In short, I like most barbeque and the side orders that come with it.

Ambience matters. For whatever mysterious reason, the meal tastes best when eaten in a room full of mismatched tables and folding chairs with sawdust on the floor, or outdoors under a canvas tarp on wooden benches with dirt beneath your feet. Rolls of paper towels are preferable to napkins and listings of the daily fare on chalkboards trump printed menus. Ludlow Porch,[39] a Georgia humorist, once devoted an entire radio broadcast to encouraging his listeners to describe the features (e.g., red-and-white checked oilcloth table

---

39 Ludlow Porch (1934–2011), born Bobby Crawford Hanson, was the author of many humor books, including *Fat White Guys Cookbook* and *Who Cares about Apathy?* Unlike his stepbrother, Lewis Grizzard, another humorist whose comedy could be a bit offensive and derogatory, Ludlow's gentle style encouraged folks to laugh at themselves and the general human condition.

coverings) that distinguished great barbeque joints.

My ruminations were interrupted when we spotted a hand-lettered sign on the right advertising barbeque. We turned and drove into the town of Lumpkin, the government center of Stewart County (population: 6,000+ inhabitants; that's the county, not the town). And there, in the center of town, at the intersection of Cotton and West Broad Streets with a single blinking red light, stood the simply but aptly named 4WayBbq.

We pulled into the lot behind the large old house (which doubled as restaurant and home for the owners) and found a parking space. Around us was a variety of old pick-up trucks with the obligatory gun racks and Confederate battle flag decals in the rear windows of their cabs. The place was understaffed that day, so the indoor dining room was closed. We hollered our order through an open front window and found a place to sit on the wide porch. As we waited for what turned out to be reasonably good food, Linda turned the menu upside down and spotted the slogan that would seal the 4WayBbq in our memory forever:

OUR BUTTS SMELL GOOD.

"Mornin'!"

Sure, it's probably a carefully calculated part of the customer relations strategy. Still, it feels mighty comforting on a cold morning to walk up to that yellow and Black building with its steamed-over windows, to push open the door, and to be welcomed by a chorus of "mornin's" from a team of smiling short-order cooks and wait staff.

I don't recall where or when I first stepped into a Waffle House. However, I don't think I have taken a trip anywhere in the South during the past five decades without frequenting at least one of the franchises. This chain of culinary comfort has been growing since the founders opened the first one in Avondale Estates on the outskirts of Atlanta in 1955. The last time I researched the subject, I learned that there are about 2,100 Waffle Houses in twenty-five states—more than four hundred in Georgia alone. As best I can tell, that means I've visited at least ten percent of them and stopped many times at the ones on my regular routes.[40]

Because my taste buds gravitate toward savory items, I have never ordered a waffle. However, there have been many times when I would happily have crawled over broken glass to get a plate of fried eggs "over easy," patty sausage, and hash browns.

In fact, I'd settle for only the hash browns. I don't know of any other diner in the world that serves them in as many ways. Since much of the Waffle House operation is based on code, let me spell out the options: scattered hash browns (just spread on the grill and heated); smothered (with onions); covered (with cheese); chunked

---

40 *https://wafflehouse.com* for this citation and other information about the company.

(with diced ham); diced (with diced tomatoes); peppered (with jalapeño peppers); capped (with mushrooms); topped (with chili); all the way (a self-explanatory taste riot of all those ingredients). I noticed on a menu recently that hash browns are now available "country" style—with sausage gravy poured over them!

Waffle House claims to serve two percent of all the eggs dished up in the United States. I wouldn't bet against that assertion. It further boasts that it sells more waffles, ham, pork chops, grits, and T-bone steaks than anyone else. Again, no argument from me.

The apron-ed cooks and servers come in all shapes, sizes, and skin hues, as revealed in part by their name tags: Mae, Shaniqua, Louise, Aisha, Peggy, Yolanda, Vicki, Lori, Tammi (names that end with "i" seem popular). Not a lot of Megans or Tiffanys or Madisons or Caitlins in the lineup. Maybe somewhere in the chain they have male waiters, but I have always been served by women; conversely, most of the cooks whom I've encountered are men.

Because orders are cooked separately, what comes off the grill may vary. The omelet at the Waffle House at the Anniston, Alabama turnoff from I-20 may be fluffier than the one at the Forest City, Arkansas, exit off I-40. The texture of the grits in Dublin, Georgia, might be different from the consistency of the ones in the north Georgia mountain town of Clayton. (Could it have anything to do with the altitude?) Standards don't necessarily assure rigid uniformity.

The crowning achievement on the diversity front at Waffle House is the company's clientele. By staying open twenty-four hours a day (contrary to legend, the doors do have locks), seven days a week, they attract the entire range of the population. African Americans, whites, Hispanics, and international visitors. Travelers blowing through from Lincoln, Nebraska on their way to Sarasota, Florida. The four heavyset, older guys in bib overalls who squeeze into the same booth every morning for coffee and breakfast before going to work. The long-distance trucker who takes a seat at the counter after getting his rig's gas tank filled at the pumps across the parking lot. Teenagers who've been to a late-night concert and elderly couples stopping for lunch on their way home from church.

Good corporate citizen that it is, the company has an elaborate behind-the-scenes mechanism to respond to natural disasters that includes the positioning of portable generators, food, and ice ahead of severe weather. The ability of a local Waffle House to remain open or re-open after a severe storm, even if only with a limited menu, is used by FEMA (the Federal Emergency Management Agency) as a measure of disaster recovery. It's known as (what else?) the Waffle House Index.

In a time of rapid change, when some folks worry that the South may have lost some of its better nature, praise be for a cultural icon that continues to bind and unify us.

Manuel's Tavern

For a regular patron, a great time (not that there's ever a bad time) to arrive at Manuel's Tavern in Atlanta, one of my all-time favorite watering holes, is between 4 and 5 p.m. The waitstaff is changing shifts, and the evening rush hasn't yet started. If I'm by myself, I can find a stool at the long bar or, if someone will be joining me, I can slide into one of the battered old wooden booths. Either way, the bartender who knows my preferences will have seen me enter the room and have my drink in front of me by the time I'm seated.

Manuel's reminds me of the old neighborhood bars in Northern cities that function as virtual community centers—places where "everybody knows your name." Roche and O'Brien's on Lancaster Avenue in Haverford, Pennsylvania, is like that. The first time I returned there, several *years* after graduating from college, the bartender, greeted me with, "You want the usual, Martin?"

Manuel's has one other piece of *lagniappe* that sets it apart from other eateries and pubs. Directly behind the back entrance are two parking spaces labeled: "CLERGY PARKING ONLY" (Seriously!). The story I've been told is that a priest (or maybe it was a bishop) of the Orthodox Church to which Manuel belonged came by for a meal but was miffed because the spot he found in the parking lot was too far from the door to suit him. Manuel's solution: give the clergy their own parking spot.

I have a master's degree in divinity from an accredited seminary but chose not to be ordained after graduation. Years ago, though, at the encouragement of a friend, I followed his lead and sent $9.95 to the Universal Life Church to acquire that certification. (It's not the same thing as sanctification!) The new parking arrangement at Manuel's prompted me to get back in touch with my mail order alma mater and request a clergy identification tag to hang from my car's rearview mirror. (It cost more than the ordination.) Thus equipped, I feel completely justified in grabbing one of those convenient spaces whenever it's available.

Atlanta has no shortage of drinking establishments for both its own mushrooming population and the thousands of conventioneers who throng our city on a regular basis, but I submit that there is nothing like Manuel's. It was established in 1956 by Manuel Maloof, the tough-talking son of Lebanese immigrants. He also was a significant local politician who eventually became CEO of the DeKalb County Commission. The eponymous tavern continues to be a favored gathering place for other politicians, reporters, community activists, and academics, as well as contractors, day laborers, secretaries, and telephone repairmen. People pay for their drinks with both platinum American Express cards and crumpled bills.

Manuel cagily located what initially was just a neighborhood establishment close to the boundary of Fulton County (which permitted the sale of alcoholic beverages) and DeKalb County (which was dry). He thereby won the undying loyalty of professors and students from Emory University, Agnes Scott College, and Columbia Theological Seminary by providing them easy access to otherwise forbidden pleasures.

Manuel, who died in 2004 at the age of eighty, made no secret of his political allegiances. Centered behind the bar is a painting of John F. Kennedy, and around that portrait hang Black and white photographs and pictures of FDR, Hubert Humphrey (allegedly Manuel's personal hero), and Lyndon Johnson. Look further for pictures of the Clintons, the Gores, the Carters, Sam Nunn, and Andrew Young. There is a photograph of Ralph McGill, columnist at *The Atlanta Constitution*, and a large one of Manuel, his wife, and the first of seven children. During his later years, Manuel would sit on a stool behind the bar, ordering his family members and other employees around and dispensing political wisdom to all within the sound of his raspy voice.

For many years, Manuel's was simply a tavern, offering beer and sandwiches, and we regulars were worried when it obtained a license to serve mixed drinks. However, the effeteness that we thought might follow never materialized, and even the expansion of the menu to include hearty appetizers, good steaks, seafood, and other dinner items never threatened the ambience. It also has its own good house brew (the "602") on tap. A few video games can be found on the way to the restrooms, and the cash register, beside which stands an unused spittoon, has been replaced by a computer, but there aren't many other concessions to modernity. The faded sports pennants, the collection of German beer steins, and a host of other souvenirs are still behind the bar, as is the scale model of a Budweiser beer wagon being pulled by eight Clydesdales. So are the urns containing the ashes of Manuel and others close to the establishment.

A while back, the current generation of the tavern's owners closed the place down for the better part of a year for renovations. Before doing so, they carefully photographed the entire interior so that all the photos, paintings, and artifacts could be returned to their places when the work was done. When Manuel's re-opened, we could hardly tell the difference. Behind the scenes, the kitchen had been greatly expanded and the bathrooms rebuilt and refurbished—a welcome change. Otherwise, except for smelling noticeably cleaner, Manuel's was still Manuel's . . . and so it remains.

Relearning How to Tell Time

Until Henry Louis Gates, Jr. pulls out his genealogical tables and DNA charts and informs me otherwise, I will continue to live with the conviction that I am genetically one hundred percent German. My mother's family has lived for centuries in a small village in Thuringia, whose church was built as a Roman Catholic sanctuary long before the Reformation. My father's ancestral line, according to a chart that a family member proudly shared with me, can be traced back to Charlemagne. To be sure, as a cynical young cousin once snorted disparagingly, "Do the math; everybody's related to Charlemagne." Nonetheless, although it may be inappropriate to refer to the Holy Roman Emperor crowned in 800 as Uncle Charlie, I consider myself to be a thoroughly Teutonic figure.

I go into all that probably unnecessary detail to make a point. Because of those genes, I am basically hardwired to be on time for all occasions to which I am invited. As a result, it took years to surmount the cultural clash involved when I went to social occasions hosted by African American friends.

If memory serves correctly, my compulsive punctuality first became an issue at a party hosted by the Clark College president soon after I joined the administrative staff. The invitation noted that the event would begin at 7 p.m. At 6:58, I parked the car at the curb in front of his home, led my wife to the front entrance, and rang the buzzer. A member of the family opened the door and stared at us as if we might be Jehovah's Witnesses or magazine salespeople. Once we established that ours was a social call, we were invited into the living room.

Our host appeared in shirt sleeves and stockinged feet and welcomed us genially, although it was clear that he too couldn't believe that we were already there. He hollered to his wife that they had guests. She appeared and, giggling a bit, said, in effect, "You need to learn a bit more about us." African Americans, she further explained, invariably arrive later than the appointed hour because they operate on C(olored) P(eople) time.

Over the coming weeks, and months, and years, I tried to curb my DNA-driven impulses to operate on white (or, perhaps more correctly, "German") time. With conscious effort I managed to show up five minutes, then ten minutes, then twenty minutes "late." I eventually discovered that I could appear a half-hour after the stated beginning time of an event and still be among the first people in attendance. I have resigned myself to this failing, and my hosts have learned to tolerate my foreign ways.

"Don't Be Ugly!"

I asked my older daughter—raised in the South through high school but since then a resident of Wisconsin, Indiana, and finally Ohio—what she thought was one of the most telling differences between the South and North. Liz barely pondered the question. "Politeness," she swiftly answered—meaning, to be clear, that Southerners have better manners.

Despite agreeing, I pushed her a bit, "But when Southerners are courteous, isn't it sometimes phony?"

"Of course," she matter-of-factly replied.

As her response indicated, it is true that civility can mask honesty, but it can also ward off an escalation of bad temper. A long-time friend and colleague, the recently retired head of a private foundation, was a master of this technique. When someone would disagree with him, Frank simply chuckled and replied, "Well, you may be right." It was a most disarming response that had the added benefit at times of leaving his would-be combatant sputtering.

Liz and I went on to share a variety of related observations. We noted that most children raised in the South respond to questions and requests from their elders by saying, "Yes, ma'am" or "Yes, sir." They ask with a "please" and receive with a "thank you."

I was once asked to appear on a panel to respond to the author of a book with whose opinions I was in almost total disagreement. Preparing to leave for the program, I ran through my critical and rather argumentative notes one last time. As I headed out the door, Linda, my kindly Southern spouse, looked up from what she was doing and said quietly, "Now don't be ugly." She was correct in trying to curb my less-than-charitable remarks. By the time I reached the auditorium, I had toned them down and was able to conduct myself with a measure of civility. On other similar occasions, she has offered an alternative bit of caution: "Be sweet, now!"

A friend and classmate at graduate school in New York was a gentle, kind, thoughtful person—Southern born, bred, and educated. As several of us were engaged in conversation one day, I uttered a typically boorish and uncouth remark. (Remember, these were the days when I was still a coarse and offensive Yankee.)

Ruth immediately responded, "Oh, Martin. That is so tacky!"

I had never heard the expression and so had no idea that it is one of the most dismissive adjectives in a Southerner's lexicon. I have since sought the origin of the word and learned that it is derived from the name of a small horse bred in the South in the nineteenth century—the Carolina Marsh Tacky (of which only a few remain). Anyway, the term evolved from a noun to a versatile adjective with many synonyms: graceless, tactless, rude, unpolished, inelegant, unrefined, ill-bred. In other words, to do or say something tacky is to demonstrate a lack of sensitivity and class.

However, bear in mind that to be tacky has nothing to do with one's station in life. Being poor or uneducated does not necessarily make one tacky. On the other side of that equation are plenty of highly placed and wealthy individuals who are the epitome of tackiness.

In the South, people speak when spoken to. If people (yes, even strangers) encounter each other, one of them is expected to say, "Hello," or "Hey," or "Good morning," and the other responds in kind. If you want to scare New Yorkers to death when you pass them on the sidewalk, offer a word of greeting. They will avert their eyes, and their pace will immediately quicken as they seek to distance themselves from you. If you address a comment to the Yankee with whom you are alone in an elevator, that person may pull out a can of mace or, to quote Travis Bickle from the movie *Taxi Driver*, growl, "You talkin' to me?"

When greeting a friend or acquaintance, it is also most appropriate to inquire about their kinfolk; a customary query in parts of the South is "How's your momma 'n' 'em?"

Another conversational gambit I had to learn involved the matter of talking "bidness." Before shedding my Yankee habits, I would show up for an appointment and immediately dive into the purpose for the visit. Now, of course, I understand that this approach is thoroughly gauche: first, one should dispense with equally or more important subjects like family, health, or the previous night's nationally televised football game—thereby granting the other party the respect they are due.

The sum of my learning may be that paying attention to the seemingly "ordinary" elements of life can help us set a good tempo and rhythm for all our behavior. There is great value in taking the time to determine both our common understandings and the quirky differences that set us apart and make us interesting before we plunge into the often-combative world of ideals, ideas, and just plain biases. We do well to give ourselves the time and space to listen, watch, and learn before being too quick to assume we understand our fellow citizens. I still haven't fully mastered the technique, but I don't think I would have learned this lesson as well anywhere else but the South.

"Have a Blessed Day."

When I began my travels in the South, many restaurants advertised that they would give free desserts with Sunday lunch to any customers who could display bulletins from their church's morning worship services. Sunday morning television then consisted primarily of live church services and taped programs of the Statler Brothers and other white male quartets singing gospel songs in close harmony. Almost all commercial establishments were closed then, and it was impossible to buy an alcoholic beverage.

Those days are gone. A growing number of folks—especially urban Southerners—head for coffeehouses, dog parks, soccer fields, and Wal-Marts when the church bells ring on Sunday morning.[41]

Times have changed, to be sure, but what I want to highlight here is that lots of people in the South still go to church—sometimes twice a week. That's a fact. They also attend worship services at synagogues and mosques and Hindu temples and Baha'i centers. For the moment, though, I want to focus on the ones who prompted H. L. Mencken to describe us as the Bible Belt.

Further proof of my assertions about churchgoing can be found at the Cracker Barrel that is nearest to any small town in the South, between noon and one o'clock on a Sunday. The line of Baptists waiting to eat lunch stretches into the parking lot. Yes, ours is still a religious region.

---

41 The truly remarkable exception in our commercially driven society is Chick-fil-A. Its refusal to open for business on Sundays, Thanksgiving, or Christmas is based on the values of its devout, Southern Baptist founders. Beginning as a single restaurant in Hapeville, Georgia in 1946, it rebranded itself in 1967 and went on to become one of our country's most profitable restaurant chains.

Here's other evidence to support that contention:

- In the South, politicians feel comfortable sprinkling their speeches with Biblical quotes. They can assume that their listeners memorized those same verses in Sunday school and immediately recognize the allusions.
- Store clerks—especially African American employees—still conclude transactions by telling their customers, "Have a blessed day." It's not exactly a pastoral benediction, but I find it to be a reassuring statement of support. It's altogether different from "Bless your heart," which is a pleasantly pitying way to tell other people that they're sadly mistaken or maybe even full of s***.
- Upon introduction, it is natural for perfect strangers to ask new acquaintances where they go to church . . . and to invite them to their own houses of worship if they don't receive a definitive answer.
- Only in the South: when a touchy situation would benefit from further frank discussion and resolution, someone will declare, "It's time for a 'come to Jesus' meeting."
- A useful litmus test of a public religious figure's true character has to do with the tears he or she sheds in a televised plea for forgiveness after having been exposed as a crook, an adulterer, or a liar. Southerners love noisily repentant fallen angels and soon will be sending donations their way again.

I need to stress that what I am describing primarily relates to white churchgoers. Lots of Black folks pack the pews too, but most of them have different experiences. Martin Luther King, Jr. was correct when he described the time between 11 and 12 o'clock on Sunday mornings as being the most racially segregated hour in America. But that separation is not solely the result of prejudice. White Presbyterians (sometimes known as "God's frozen chosen") and Episcopalians, for example, simply have never learned to sing and praise the Lord with the same joyful abandon as many an African American congregation. And if white American Christians don't hear their minister pronounce the benediction by noon, they are not likely to continue their membership in that church.

For some white Southerners, their faith is best captured in eclectically blended iconography that easily unites faith, history, memory, and popular culture. I call the reader's attention to a painting that is perhaps the most emblematic piece of regional ecclesiastical art. Painted by Clyde Broadway, Jr. in 1994, its title is simply "Trinity." This unique acrylic-on-canvas work that measures thirty-seven by forty-nine inches with a gold leaf border portrays the figure of Jesus with Elvis Presley (holding a guitar) to his right, and Robert E. Lee on his left. The three figures stand on a bed of roses with blooming magnolia blossoms above them.[42]

Then again, perhaps it would be more accurate to characterize us as a pious region. I looked up the word "piety," and learned that one of its definitions focuses upon the act of religiously correct behavior. In the South, superficial religiosity is not necessarily phony. It's hard to explain, but, after many years, it all seems natural to me.

There's one other custom I need to identify, even though I'm not completely sure whether it belongs in a roster of preferred religious behavior. It involves pulling over to the side of the road and stopping while a funeral procession passes. Clearly it is not required by the Ten Commandments, but several Southern states mandate it in their traffic laws.

Many people in my neighborhood still extend this sign of respect for the deceased and the deceased's family when a funeral procession travels slowly up Cascade Road, but it is a vanishing observance in most urban areas. In small towns and rural sections, though, not steering one's car to the shoulder of the road when a line of cars with shining headlights approaches (preceded by a cop

---

42 The last time I checked, the painting was on display at the Ogden Museum of Southern Art at 925 Camp Street in New Orleans.

on a motorcycle) is a sure way to be labeled as a foreigner or a heathen or even a lawbreaker.

Ours is also a region that is rich in ambivalence and ambiguity. It may well be true that lots of congregations would proudly lay claim to being the buckle on that biblical belt. And many of their members grew up with the King James Version of the Bible and memorized all the words of Jesus—easily identified because they were printed in red ink. But, sad to say, a lot of these folks have limited recall. Once out the door of the sanctuary, the relevance of instructions like the Golden Rule and the Sermon on the Mount seems to lose a lot of its kick. Up North, far fewer people are religious believers, so they don't even realize the extent of their transgressions. I'm still trying to figure out whether I prefer atheists or hypocrites.

Tempted to stray from the path of righteousness? Pay attention to the words of a song that's been around for a long time and gets re-recorded periodically, "Get in touch with God, turn your radio on (and listen to the music in the air. . . .").[43]

Which leads me to note that there are some powerful gospel hymns that capture the full depth of grace-filled Protestantism. I know that my next claim will generate angry responses, but there also are as many gospel hymns that are theologically skimpy, vapid, non-Biblical and artificially sentimental.[44] Nonetheless, take the words of those songs, often packed with questionable theological concepts, set them to music, harmonize those gory images of Jesus on a cross and warble that his daddy put him there to save our sins,

---

43 Composed in 1939 by Albert E. Brumley and first recorded by Lulu Belle & Scotty and Five String Banjo.

44 As a mild example, I offer "That Old Time Religion." Its authorship is uncertain, and people keep adding verses to the original text. I read somewhere that it was first sung in public by the Jubilee Singers of Fisk University, who went on the road seven years after the Civil War to raise money for their institution. It is fun to sing, but one won't have to study the text too carefully to realize that it does a better job of conveying emotion than capturing clear thinking. We never do find out exactly what that old time religion was. One thing is certain though: it was not only good for the Hebrew children and Paul and Silas and our grandparents, but even for us. A strong runner-up on any list of theologically questionable favorites begins, "Life is Like a Mountain Railroad."

throw in some images of fountains filled with blood and self-flag-ellation, and I'm likely to have tears running down my cheeks as I sing along.

To conclude this rambling, let me suggest a litmus test of sorts that may help to figure out where one might fit on the appreciation spectrum for this branch of religious hymnody: Head over to the Elvis Presley birthplace park, east of downtown Tupelo, Mississippi, early on some frosty morning while the mist is still rising from the lawn and before too many visitors begin to gather. There's a small chapel in the museum with a plate glass window that overlooks Elvis's first two-room, shotgun home with a swing on the porch. (The place is much more gussied up with gleaming white paint than when he lived there.) Settle into a pew and listen to the recorded voice of the King singing "Peace in the Valley."[45] Anyone for whom that doesn't produce a lump in the throat, may indeed not be from these parts.

---

45 Written for Mahalia Jackson by Thomas A. Dorsey, the composer of some three thousand hymns (e.g., "Precious Lord, Take My Hand"). Dorsey ("father" of modern gospel music), Edwin Hawkins ("Oh Happy Day"), and Richard Smallwood ("Total Praise") are but three of the African American hymn writers whose works are a source of comfort and joy to many.

Part Three
REGIONAL RAMBLING

An Autobiographical Interruption

Several readers of this manuscript have suggested that I insert a few words about the rest of my career after my initial years at Clark College. I'll try to keep it brief.

After Vivian Henderson's death, I went to work for the Atlanta University Center, the consortium to which Clark belonged. My principal assignment was to coordinate a campaign for a new ten-million-dollar central library to serve the member institutions. Primarily because of the personal financial support of Robert W. Woodruff, the former chairman of the Coca-Cola Company, the project was successful.

With the handsome new library rising from the ground along Chestnut Street[46] in 1982, it seemed a good time for me to move on. But in what direction? Upward advancement was blocked; no one was going to make me the chancellor of a Black university complex. I also wasn't aware of any new project or not-for-profit job openings in Atlanta that looked interesting.

The answer to my dilemma surfaced when M. Carl Holman, President of the National Urban Coalition (and a former Clark College professor) offered me a position as fundraising consultant to his organization. It was a good experience, and I loved traveling to the nation's capital on a regular basis (and even getting to shake hands with President Carter at the White House on one occasion).

However, although it whetted my appetite for playing the role of the outside expert, I had yet to discover that consultancies are not the same as long-term salaried positions. When it be-

---

46 Soon thereafter to be christened James P. Brawley Drive.

came time to end the relationship, I suddenly realized that I should have been spending a portion of my time drumming up new business. I was once again unemployed. This time it was the Southern Presbyterian denomination that came to my temporary rescue with a new assignment.

As I think back on those days, it is transparently clear that I had never been hardwired to turn a buck. I had become adept at raising money for other people's institutions and causes, but I naïvely thought I was doing well financially if I could pay my own family's bills. The idea of generating a surplus was almost totally foreign to me. After all, in a minister's home, the operative word was spelled p-r-o-p-h-e-t.

I began by working from my home. My office was a seventy-square-foot corner of the den in a house that also was occupied by several cats—not the ideal place to invite prospective clients. I also discovered that those yellow legal tablets and pens and paper clips that had never been farther away than my employer's supply closet were now items that I had to purchase. Ever since those start-up days four decades ago, I find it impossible to attend a conference or meeting without helping myself to as many of the sponsor's or hotel's free ball point pens and note pads as I can stuff into my briefcase.

There also was the matter of getting incorporated (i.e., going through the legal fiction of making myself president of myself). I had no money for counsel. I asked a good friend and attorney with the Alston, Miller & Gaines firm for advice. Rick von Unwerth recalled that the partnership several years earlier had put a summer intern to work constructing a template for small business incorporation. For $250, he could make Lehfeldt and Associates, Inc. a legitimate company and I could claim this highly regarded law firm (now Alston + Bird) as my legal representative. Since I never would have been able to afford their services, it seems just as well that I never had to call upon them.

Slowly but steadily, other clients contracted with Lehfeldt

and Associates, Inc.[47] for our services. For a while I seemed to be typecast as the white guy who helped Black colleges raise money. Among the institutions I assisted with campaigns were LeMoyne-Owen College (Memphis, TN), Stillman College (Tuscaloosa, AL), Talladega College (Talladega, AL), and Xavier University (New Orleans, LA). We also consulted with Philander Smith College (Little Rock, AR) and Bethune-Cookman College (Daytona Beach, FL). Before the eighteen-year run of self-employment ended, we had worked with not-for-profit clients in Atlanta as well as other parts of Georgia, Alabama, Arkansas, Florida, Louisiana, South Carolina, Tennessee, Virginia, West Virginia, and Washington, DC, and then Connecticut, Michigan, New Jersey, New York, Rhode Island, and Wisconsin.

Fundraisers are the butt of almost as much disdain as lawyers. I once was told that every fundraiser should have a brother who was a pimp, so he would have someone to look up to. And then there was that fundraising colleague of mine who could never bring himself to admit to his mother what he did for a living. That dear woman finally died, still content in the knowledge that her son's profession was playing piano in a bordello.

Nasty aspersions aside, I thoroughly enjoyed separating people from a portion of their wealth and directing it toward the needs of those less fortunate. My hero since boyhood had always been Robin Hood.

About halfway through the Lehfeldt & Associates years, my clientele shifted abruptly. The opportunity to conduct (with my colleague, Dan Joslyn) a three-year evaluation of a multi-million-dollar program of the Council on Foundations in Washington, DC, led me into the world of community foundations and regional associations of grant-makers around the country. Another major shift occurred when the Southeastern Council of Foundations retained me to direct a new program to promote the establish-

---

47 Over the years, the "associates" included Elaine Nachman, Chris Starr, Nancy Roth Remington, Gloria Steele, Steve Bacon, Charles Ballance, Jack Halsell, Dan Joslyn, Michael Morgan, and Nancy Grove.

ment and strengthening of community foundations throughout the South.

My second wife, Ann Ashford, was a gifted cook, storyteller, actress, and stepmother. Even as my professional scope of work expanded, her creativity reached a new peak, and she achieved a measure of fame as the author of *If I Found a Wistful Unicorn*.[48] Beautifully illustrated, this whimsical poem launched Peachtree Publishers in Atlanta and soon had Ann in demand for book signings and other appearances. However, close to our sixteenth wedding anniversary in 1988, while both of our children were still in college, she succumbed to the return and metastasis of a nasty form of breast cancer. Some eighteen months later, I married Linda Graham Knight, a member of my church whom I first met in 1972, and Kari Love Knight became my stepdaughter. After more than thirty years, Linda and I continue to keep each other company.

On January 1, 1998, I became President and CEO of the Southeastern Council of Foundations (an organization, interestingly, that had come into being the same year I moved to the South). I had spent most of the previous twenty-eight years helping people to raise money. Now I was getting a shot at advising grant-makers about how to run their affairs in an orderly and ethical fashion and to give money away intelligently. The shift from being a supplicant and rising from my knees to become a friend of the donors was a pleasant turn of affairs.

Throughout the next eleven years, we added a lot of programs and services for the members, greatly expanded and diversified the staff, collaborated with other regional associations of grant-makers and the national Council on Foundations, and earned ourselves some national visibility and leadership. Many of the details about our activities can be found in the previously cited *The Liberating Promise of Philanthropy* that Jamil Zainaldin and I completed in 2019.

While the CEO, I tried to remain professionally neutral about

---

48 Forty-four years after first appearing, the book remains in print and continues to delight new generations of readers.

what our members should support. Years earlier, the association had intentionally thrown up a large tent under which all sorts of foundations and giving programs were welcome. We had a member foundation that supported genealogical research and another that worked to protect the bald eagle. One member only made capital grants to colleges and universities. Others supported programs to protect the environment, to promote social justice, and to empower the disenfranchised. Many were general purpose foundations that were willing to consider a wide variety of proposals. All these missions are laudable. I remain convinced that it would be ill-informed and even dangerous to take away the independence of any of our nation's private foundations.

So, what is the purpose of foundations? A perfectly acceptable answer, as far as I'm concerned, is that they exist to serve the public good. The healthy debates begin when people try to reach consensus about what constitutes "the public good."

My philosophically egalitarian position did not dissuade me from volunteering my thoughts about what I considered to be the best kind of philanthropy. Those members who did not appreciate my frankness (which often surfaced in a monthly newsletter column) described it as "Martin's gettin' to meddlin' again."

When the time came to retire, I was perhaps proudest that the board, the members, the staff, and I together had broadened the impact of the organization, promoted greater diversity, and encouraged increased professionalism and accountability without losing the "family" ethos for which the Southeastern Council was nationally recognized.

One of the greatest personal gifts that came with the "job" was the opportunity to roam through the states of Alabama, Arkansas, Florida, Georgia, Kentucky, Louisiana, Mississippi, North Carolina, South Carolina, Tennessee, Virginia, and West Virginia. In so doing, I got to know literally hundreds of grant-making foundations and thousands of their board and staff members.

When History Met Philanthropy

The last annual meeting of the Southeastern Council of Foundations over which Bob Hull, my predecessor as SECF President, would preside was to be held at the grand old Peabody Hotel in Memphis in 1997. As November neared, the planning committee still had not identified a keynote speaker. Hampering their efforts was the council's tradition of not paying significant honoraria—sometimes travel expenses would be covered, but not budget-busting speaker fees. Bob, though, was desperate and finally decided to break with precedent. He estimated that he would be able to find $5,000 in the SECF budget to compensate a keynoter.

He next placed a call to Shelby Foote. Foote was the novelist and historian who had achieved a measure of national stardom from his appearance on Ken Burns's award-winning television series about the Civil War. He lived in Memphis.

After Hull explained the situation, Foote explained that he normally did not make speeches. He was about to bring the conversation to an end when Hull let it be known that the assignment carried with it a modest honorarium. Foote quickly requested a definition of "modest." When Hull named the figure, Foote "allowed as how" he could make himself available after all.

When the appointed hour arrived, so did Mr. Foote. However, it was soon apparent that he had not foregone the opportunity to quaff a few adult beverages before his appearance at the Peabody. He wasn't outrageously inebriated, and his eyes still had the twinkle that had helped to endear him to television audiences, but they looked a bit glazed.

After being introduced, he stood up and offered several provocative insights about the Civil War and Reconstruction that held promise of leading into a first-rate speech. But then he seemingly remembered that he was addressing a roomful of foundation trustees and administrators. Without benefit of any segue, he switched gears and launched into a series of anecdotes about receiving a fellowship for research and study from a well-known, national philanthropic institution. His eyes now twinkling most merrily, he reported that he had used his stipend to rent a home in the Georgetown section of Washington, DC, and spent the rest of it on alcoholic refreshment. Looking sternly at the audience, he concluded, "I think y'all need to approach your work very carefully," and stepped away from the lectern. His body language made it clear that he had nothing further to say. The entire presentation had lasted perhaps ten minutes.

It was left to Katharine Pearson, the SECF chairperson, to extemporize an expression of appreciation for Mr. Foote's comments. He shook a few more hands and then vanished. The rest of us, finding ourselves with an hour or so of unexpected free time before the next scheduled conference session, went shopping, visited the coffee shop, or repaired to the grand lobby bar and watched the mallard ducks swimming in the marble fountain.

Brand Loyalty

Until I came South, a preference for any particular carbonated beverage was a matter of almost complete indifference to me. The cash-strapped household in which I grew up couldn't afford any of those beverages. We purchased little envelopes of flavored powder for a nickel apiece and mixed them with water and sugar. My first girlfriend swore by the superiority of a brand that will go nameless in this sketch and drank it incessantly, but even love could not make me a convert—nor did I have any other favorite.

Then I moved to Atlanta, the headquarters city of Coca-Cola (pronounces "co-cola") Here there is only one real thing, and it often appears that Coca-Cola and its derivatives dominate the drinking habits of the entire region.

As hard as it may be to believe, there are parts of the South in which Coca-Cola is not the principal soft drink. Here and there, I have heard tell, competing bubbly and fruit-flavored brands appear on supermarket shelves, in vending machines, and on restaurant menus.

However, that doesn't stop the producer of the pause that refreshes from battling for every competitive advantage, assisted by consumers whose devotion to it is fanatical.

The founders of a significant number of the Southeastern Council of Foundations' members owed their multi-million-dollar endowments to the wisdom of having purchased Coca-Cola stock during that company's early years and hanging on to it. The following story, related to me by my predecessor, Bob Hull, soon after I came to SECF, illustrates the power and pervasiveness of the world of Coca-Cola.

The Southeastern Council holds an annual meeting each November, rotating it around the region. One year, Bob invited some of the conference attendees to his suite for a small reception. As he told the story, the head of a foundation whose portfolio was composed almost entirely of Coca-Cola stock was one of the guests. Upon entering the room, he walked over to the bar to fix himself a drink. There he discovered that all the mixers displayed were manufactured by Coca-Cola competitors. Without uttering a word, he quietly opened all the bottles, poured their contents down the drain, and called room service to restock the bar with Coca-Cola products.

Having heard that story, I quickly made product loyalty a key tenet of my faith. Thereafter, I was on guard to prevent a similar snafu from occurring on my watch; indeed, we had it written into all future contracts with every conference hotel that only one company's brands could be served at any of our functions.

What can I say? We believe in dancing with the one who brought us to the party.

Life in the Conch Republic

On those days when the workload is especially onerous, or the weather outside is frightful, or the world seems to be going straight to hell, my thoughts invariably turn to the Florida Keys. That idiosyncratic part of the world, also known as the Conch Republic,[49] is for me a symbol of escape and freedom.

I have fond memories of my first encounter years ago with that distant colony. Linda flew down from Atlanta to meet me at a conference I was attending in Miami. The next day, under a bright, sunny sky, we drove along the single-lane highway that crosses a one-hundred-mile stretch of islands, bridges, and causeways till we reached the southernmost point of the United States.

On that trip, we strolled everywhere. We visited the Ernest Hemingway house with its unrestrained colony of six-toed cats, and had a drink at Sloppy Joe's, the famous author's favorite bar. We also wandered through the cemetery with the tombstone of the infamous hypochondriac on which are etched her immortal words: "I told you I was sick." The operative dress code for the people we passed was distinctly countercultural, and the passersby we encountered exhibited more bare skin than fabric.

Among the many laid-back images of the place that I recall, one stands out. When the day came to an end, residents and tourists alike thronged to Mallory Square to watch the sun set. Street performers and vendors abounded. Everyone—not just the folks

---

49 Marine biologists define conchs as a form of gastropods—sea-dwelling mollusks whose flesh can be cooked and eaten. Conchs also are those people whose ancestors "seceded" from the State of Florida on April 23, 1982.

smoking pot—seemed mellow. As the gleaming reddish-gold ball fell below the horizon, people cheered. I have read an account which claims that Tennessee Williams was the first person to begin clapping at the sight, thereby inaugurating this tradition. It might be true.

In that milieu we encountered a "salesman" of indeterminate age with shoulder-length hair and a beard. His only attire was a pair of cut-off jeans. No shirt, no shoes. He had a single product: refrigerator magnets, displayed on a stiff board. They were constructed of colorful seashells glued to small pieces of painted wood. Each item had "KEY WEST" neatly lettered on the front. He was selling these works of folk art for two or three dollars apiece. Of course, we bought one.

Since the encounter with that nameless, barely clothed huckster, I have with envy tried to imagine his daily routine. It might well go something like this:

6:00 a.m. Rise early in small rental apartment in an old wooden boarding house, brew a small pot of coffee, and drink a cup or two.

7:00 a.m. Pull on a pair of shorts, grab a bucket, and head for the waterfront.

7:30 a.m. Patrol the beach, collecting, rinsing, and loading shells into a bucket.

10:00 a.m. Return home, sort shells, and arrange them to dry.

11:00 a.m. Fix a sandwich, finish the morning coffee, take a nap.

1:00 p.m. Assemble and glue together seashells, small wooden blocks, and magnets, and carefully hand-letter "KEY WEST" on each item. Arrange and fasten products to the display board.

4:00 p.m. Head for Mallory Square. Find a good location (preferably a wall or bench on which to sit) and set up for business.

5:00 p.m. Sell as many refrigerator magnets as possible before the sun sets and the crowd disperses.

8:00 p.m.   Pocket the day's earnings. Head for favorite non-touristy bar and restaurant for a pleasant evening with friends, fellow entrepreneurs, and other free spirits.

Surely this outline could be a schedule for happiness. It includes the opportunity to be productive—even artistic—without complex organization . . . to be profitable by virtue of low overhead . . . to streamline one's life by the elimination of written reports, tax returns, staff meetings, or complex travel schedules.

Key West took a hit when cruise ships began docking there and disgorging hordes of tourists. Their appearance stimulated a proliferation of T-shirt shops and fast-food franchises, but these sea-going vessels did not strike a fatal blow. I haven't been to Key West for several years, but I have been assured that the essential "no worries" spirit of the island remains.

That spirit, by the way, extends to the other keys. I don't know them as well, but I offer one story in evidence. When the wife of a close friend on one of those other islands died, I immediately began preparing to attend the memorial service. It was scheduled to be held in the spacious backyard of the couple's large home overlooking the Gulf of Mexico. I was astute enough to realize that a dark suit would be inappropriate garb in that informal setting. Instead, I assembled my standard preppy uniform of dark-blue blazer, light-blue Oxford shirt with button-down collar, khakis, and penny loafers—an ensemble that has served me well since I was fifteen years old. Thus attired, I boarded my flight to Miami. As I drove away from that airport in my rental car, I chided myself for not having stopped for a shoeshine, but it was too late to correct that oversight.

I arrived at my destination about an hour before the service with the intent of visiting with my bereft friend. He was clearly saddened by the loss of his wife, but he was not garbed in sackcloth and ashes. To the contrary, he was barefoot and wearing a Hawaiian shirt and a pair of tattered shorts. As the other guests began to arrive, I quickly discovered that my concerns about polished footgear had been far off the mark. Two-thirds of the guests weren't even wearing shoes. One other person showed up wearing a blue blazer. His excuse was that he was a banker.

The couple's wedding that I had attended many years before had been in a Unitarian church, so I was not expecting a great deal of ceremony for this funeral. I was not to be disappointed. Close to the appointed hour, we gathered on the patio by the swimming pool. My friend read a tribute that he had composed. After a brief period of silence and murmurs of condolence, the bar was opened, and an alcohol-laced reception ensued.

So it is sometimes, I surmise, with life—and death—in the Florida Keys.

And Then There's the Rest of Florida

Sharing my thoughts about the Florida Keys got me to thinking about the rest of the state in which I've spent a fair amount of time. As I did, I kept coming up with a scrambled set of images that don't fit well together. At times it comes across as a scattered collection of municipalities and beaches clinging to a peninsula that itself is dangling from Georgia and Alabama. As an example, it is possible to drive from Miami to Naples in a couple of hours, but they are two different worlds—and to get from one to the other involves crossing a swamp filled with semi-aquatic reptiles. Jacksonville feels like the "real" South, and so does Tallahassee, but Tallahassee doesn't have any beaches, so why go there if one is not a state legislator or a Florida State football fan?

Many Floridians (especially the ones who live south of Orlando) don't seem to think of themselves as Southerners either. And if they sound as if they came from elsewhere, they did. I submit that a lot of them are residents only in a technical sense. They own or lease properties and spend 183 days a year there to avoid paying income tax in the states that are their "real" homes.

Those places are the ones to which they return for dental visits, physicals, holidays with their families, and appointments with their accountants and financial advisors (the very ones who encouraged them to set up residences in Florida).

I was relatively late in getting to know the state. My family was not one of those Yankee clans in the era before interstate highways that would load up the car once a year and make the arduous, driving-through-the-night trek to spend their vacations in Florida. In those days, the Northeasterners went to the Atlanta coast, and the Midwesterners headed for the beaches beside the Gulf of Mexico. We went camping in New England.

We also didn't learn much about Florida in school. Ponce de Leon got a bit of coverage, to be sure, although I gather that the fountain of youth story was a fabrication. There also weren't a lot of Hollywood films set in the state. I remember *The Yearling* (which I found to be too sentimental) and *The Palm Beach Story*, a screwball comedy with snappy dialogue. I also recall Terry Moore, Robert Wagner, and Gilbert Roland in *Beneath the 12-Mile Reef*, a story about sponge fishing off the coast of the Tampa area. Terry was the one in the form-fitting toreador pants.

My favorite film with a Florida setting is probably *Key Largo*. It was made in 1948, and I didn't get to see it until many years later. According to my research, except for a couple of scenes behind the opening credits, almost none of it was filmed in the Keys.

To broaden my knowledge, I did further investigation on the internet. Here's what I learned:

- Florida's early history involving white people differs somewhat from that of the other eastern United States. Whereas the Northern and Mid-Atlantic colonies and states bear the influence of early immigration from the British Isles and Nordic Europe, it was Spanish and French explorers and conquerors who fought to establish control of the peninsula. Like most Caucasians who "discovered" the New World, they all did their best to enslave and/or exterminate the native tribes (referred to by white folks in Florida as Seminoles).

- Florida didn't join the United States until 1845, and it did so as a slave state. Thereupon its antebellum profile soon matched that of the rest of the South.

- Its climate and soil made northern Florida an ideal agricultural region for cattle ranching, cotton, and citrus farms. Further south, massive efforts began to drain the Everglades and plant sugar cane. Farmers and loggers (the region's original "crackers"), many of them from Georgia and Alabama, came to own most of the land in northern Florida and controlled the legislature at the state capital in Tallahassee.[50] Although Florida lost young men who went north to fight in the Civil War, the state escaped the destruction wrought upon its fellow Confederate states.[51] Otherwise, it too flunked Reconstruction, championed Jim Crow, and generally lagged behind the rest of the nation in its standard of living through the Great Depression.

- The building of railroads and resorts by Henry Flagler and other entrepreneurs turned tourism into an industry, and with the onset of World War II, Florida became a vital partner in the nation's military buildup. Shipbuilding, U.S. naval operations, and military aviation brought businesses, people, and dollars into the region as never before. The state's population in 1940 totaled 1.8 million people. Thereafter and for the next several decades, those numbers would double every ten years. The forces unleashed by this economic transformation, together with the development of air conditioning and mosquito control were just the prelude for the arrival of the Space Age at Cape Canaveral in 1950 and the later Disney-led creation of a new "land of enchantment."

My happiest memory of the Orlando area involves the first visit in the 1960s. I landed in a small plane at its small airport surrounded by acres and acres (make that square miles) of beautiful orange groves. The small downtown to which I taxied for my appointment looked like my image of the colonial capital of a South American

---

50 Rob Storter and Betty Savidge Briggs, *Crackers in the Glade: Life and Times in the Old Everglades* (Athens, GA, 2000).

51 Cecelia Holland, "Florida," in Stanley I. Kutler, ed., *Dictionary of American History*, Vol. 3, 385-388.

country. At the time, we ordinary human beings had no idea that Walt Disney was getting ready to transform that vast agricultural universe into never-never land.

I had visited Disneyland in California many years earlier. It was enjoyable, but I never felt the need to return, and I think I can die happily without ever having to enter the Magic Kingdom. I will confess to having attended a meeting at Epcot, but that's the closest I've been to the Mouse and his habitat. I'm told that Disney World is or once was the most popular destination for American honeymoons. Since I don't anticipate getting married again, that's another reason for not going there. I think my annoyance with the place is the sheer and exquisite artificiality of it all. Once, as we were visiting the Tower of London on a typically British, damp, dreary, November morning, Linda heard another American tourist gush in delight, "It's almost as good as Disney World." Enough said.

I've been to Orlando many times since that first visit. It does include lovely sections, but each time it seems more congested and unnatural. On the last trip for a conference, we got thoroughly lost. Despite the best efforts of our GPS, we wandered about for the better part of an hour, trying to identify our hotel in a bewilderingly tight cluster of other high-rise hostelries. During the few days we stayed there, we were afraid to leave the property for fear we'd never find our way back.

As we all know, Florida has population pockets of enormous wealth, and I've had a goodly share of encounters with some of its representatives. Perhaps my favorite story involves the day I first traveled to Palm Beach to conduct three interviews with prospective donors as part of a campaign feasibility study. Jackie Gleason had politely brushed me off on the telephone (growling, in that inimitable voice, "Sorry, I can't help you, pal"), but one interviewee was a former governor of the state and another millionaire, whose name I've forgotten, and lived in a splendid ocean-front mansion. I had the address of the third prospect but couldn't find it even after driving up and down beside the Intercoastal Waterway for nearly half an hour. It finally dawned on me that the street number I sought was for a long dock opposite the row of houses on South Lake Drive. At the end of the pier, past several large boats, was anchored a huge yacht. It was a residence of the man for whom I was searching. How huge was it? Let me put it this way: the living room in which we sat and talked was large enough to accommodate a grand piano and an electric organ and still have plenty of room for lots of other furniture.

Not to be overlooked in any discussion of Florida is the other end of the state's economic spectrum. One of the most glaring examples of Floridian poverty is Belle Glade, about forty miles from Palm Beach. Situated on the southeastern shore of Lake Okeechobee, it is at the heart of a territory that produces half of the sugar cane in the United States. In 1960 it was featured in an Edward R. Murrow documentary titled "Harvest of Shame" that highlighted the filth, despair, and grinding poverty of life for migrant farm workers. Since then, it has gone through regular cycles of exposés, improvements, and returns to pitiful conditions and public neglect. The poor treatment of migrant workers is not, to be sure, restricted to Belle Glade or Florida or even the South, but it continues to be one of the disturbing patterns of behavior in which the region excels.

Although I'm doing a poor job of conveying positive feelings about Florida, my memories do include wonderful experiences there. One is of gathering oysters on an Easter Sunday morning in the bay by St. George Island when it was still a deserted sliver of land off the gulf coast. Another is of spending the night in a suite at the opulent Fontainebleau Hotel and watching from the balcony as a full moon shone down on the ocean at Miami Beach.

Perhaps that's the problem. Florida is a collection of isolated impressions, but, in the words of Gertrude Stein, and for me at least, there's no "there" there.

Having by now alienated any Florida friends I have (or used to have), I will close by apologizing to them. I do care for them and have enjoyed visiting many of their places of abode and employment. May they continue to enjoy their lives in the Sunshine State.

Political Cartography

During the last Christmas season, we went to a holiday party at the Absalom Jones Episcopal Center in the Atlanta University Center neighborhood a few miles from our home. One of the late arrivals was a woman who told me she had not been able to find the Fair Street address on her GPS. Well, of course not. Fair Street had recently been re-named Atlanta Student Movement Boulevard to honor the young people who gave leadership to civil rights protests in the early 1960s.

That kind of politically sensitive name-changing has been going on for a long time. In a city that has raised the demolition of historic sites to an art form, we are accustomed to giving directional instructions like "Go out Peachtree to where the Sears store used to be. . . ." But how does one steer a traveler when the street names themselves have also changed?

One of the first facts of geography I had to learn upon arrival in Atlanta involved the Old Fourth Ward—the name of the city's once racially segregated district. The name of any street that ran through that sector was changed at the border during the bad old days of Reconstruction. God forbid that a white family should have to live on the same street as that inhabited by African Americans. And so, Auburn Avenue (which had been Wheat Street) changed to Luckie Street, Boulevard became Monroe, and so on once they crossed into what was whites-only territory.

When I got here, I also found it disconcerting to discover a thoroughfare still named for Nathan Bedford Forrest, Confederate general and Grand Wizard of the Ku Klux Klan. (It was soon thereafter changed to honor Ralph McGill, and Confederate Avenue recently became United Avenue.)

The steady erosion of white political power that began with Maynard Jackson's election as mayor set in motion a wave of name changes by the City Council to honor recently deceased African American leaders of the twentieth century. Not surprisingly, Hunter Street, once named for a major plantation owner of the past, became Martin Luther King, Jr. Drive several years after Dr. King's assassination. And in later years, Ralph David Abernathy's name replaced that of Confederate general John Brown Gordon. Sewell Road in southwest Atlanta was rechristened to honor Dr. Benjamin E. Mays, the truly remarkable former president of Morehouse College and mentor of Dr. King.

However, the sometimes-impatient Black political leadership hasn't always waited for death to provide a reason for a street-naming tribute. Thus, in short order (and at times while the honorees were still alive) notables from the modern Civil Rights era found their names on street corner signs—or labeling stretches of I-285, the perimeter highway that encircles Atlanta.

The city simply doesn't seem to have a clear nomenclature standard. I have watched public thoroughfares or portions thereof acquire the names of revered pastors, businesspeople, and even undertakers. At other times it seems that elected officials, like members of a mutual admiration society, have simply taken turns assigning the names of their political colleagues and personal friends to a variety of streets and avenues.

The name changing has not always been consistent; Hamilton Holmes, who helped to integrate the University of Georgia, had a major road named after him, but Charlayne Hunter-Gault, who joined him in that pioneer undertaking, was not accorded similar treatment. (Is that because she now lives in South Africa?) And please also note the glaring absence of other female names on city street signs.

I'm fairly sure that competitive alumni emotions played a role in some of the re-naming. Thus, the Atlanta City Council, after a great deal of behind-closed-doors wrangling, and by a split vote in 1985, converted Chestnut Street, which ran through the heart of the Atlanta University Center, to James P. Brawley Drive. That decision served to preserve the memory of a former Clark College president who was a contemporary of Dr. Mays, the former president of Morehouse (who, as noted, already had a street bearing his name). Other previous college presidents are possibly still waiting in line, so to speak, to be thus recognized.

African Americans are not the only figures to give their names to Atlanta's re-christened thoroughfares. Part of Simpson Road has become Ivan Allen Drive, renamed for the former mayor of Atlanta; portions of Spring Street now bear CNN founder Ted Turner's name; and architect John Portman was also thus honored by "giving" his name to a section of Harris Street.

So far, I have no quarrels with most of the street-naming selections; the people being recognized have performed meritorious public service. However, we're running out of major traffic arteries; at the rate we're going, the value of having a thoroughfare bear one's name is going to be deeply discounted. My proposal is that no roads or highways be assigned new names until the persons being thus honored are still recognized for their accomplishments in a public referendum after having been dead for at least twenty years.

Nothin' but a Hound Dog

We were returning from a visit to family in Arkansas and crossing northern Alabama on Route 72, when we spotted the crude sign with an arrow directing travelers to the National Coon Dog Cemetery. Who knew that such a memorial even existed?

It had been our goal to reach Atlanta by bedtime, but the chance to view this singular landmark was sufficiently intriguing to lure us off the highway. We are not coon dog fanciers; we couldn't even be labeled as dog lovers, since we share our residence with three cats. Nonetheless, the fact that a national monument of this kind had been established right there in Alabama hooked our imaginations. We drove down a back road in the failing light for several miles, but when no further directional markers appeared, we gave up the search—at least temporarily.

We planned our next westward trip to include a stop at this mysterious graveyard, but our second attempt to find it also came to naught. More time passed. Tales of our efforts made for a good story, but we still wanted to be able to claim to have seen the real thing. An opportunity presented itself on yet another trip to Arkansas. We were determined that our third quest for the elusive burial ground would meet with success.

The ever-expanding internet had provided us with a new set of directions. They instructed us to take a different turn off the main highway than we had followed before. We were soon in a remote portion of Colbert County, following a series of twisting, turning, and barely marked roads past fields and forests until our pilgrimage was rewarded with the sight of our long-sought destination. There it stood (in the middle of nowhere, as they say): the final resting place for Ol' Blue, Traveler, Duke, Ranger, Ruby, Scout, and other beloved hunting companions. A large statue of two dogs treeing a raccoon graced the entrance. I don't know what breed of canine Stephen Foster had in mind, but the refrain from one of his songs floated through my brain: "I'll never, never find a more faithful friend than Old Dog Tray."

All was quiet. A gentle breeze stirred the trees on this well-tended knoll. We were the only visitors at that hour. It didn't make us too nervous to hear shots being fired nearby; after all, we had passed a gun club on our way to this sacred place.

The first fact we had to absorb was the correct name of our location. As a sign made clear, we had arrived at the Ken Underwood Coon Dog Memorial Graveyard. Further research revealed that Mr. Underwood had buried his beloved companion, Troop, on this site of a former hunting club in September 1937. Over the years, other hound owners had followed his lead. More than three hundred prized canines are interred there.

Burial in this secluded necropolis is restricted. Poodle or lap dog owners need not seek space for their deceased pets. To qualify, a candidate for interment must meet three requirements. The owner must verify that the animal is a purebred; a witness must corroborate that it is a coon dog; and a member of the local coon hunters' organization must be allowed to view the remains for further confirmation.

Underwood had chiseled an old chimney stone as a grave marker for Troop that is still standing. Other headstones and plaques in the cemetery range from homemade wooden and metal monuments to more elaborate, engraved marble and granite remembrances. Many of them were decorated by bright-colored plastic flowers. Some of them had coins deposited on them as a sign of respect. We didn't have any spare change, so we simply signed the guest register to record that we had stopped to honor these deceased hunters. I felt no need to offer silent prayers or further solemnize the occasion (after all, it wasn't as if we were at the memorial garden in Graceland).

But we did stand in reverent silence for a while to salute the unique tribute to a narrowly defined slice of culture.

As we continued west toward Memphis that day, we passed a sign directing us to the National Bird Dog Museum in Grand Junction, Tennessee. After brief consideration of a detour to yet another canine memorial, we decided we had already had enough excitement for one day. But we may get there yet!

A Family Pilgrimage

Tahlequah, Oklahoma, is not a Southern town. But the community's twelve-thousand-plus inhabitants include descendants of ex-Southerners who were rounded up and force-marched here in 1838. I am referring to the infamous Trail of Tears, one among the many cruelties of white settlers to Native Americans. Today, Tahlequah is the capital of the Cherokee Nation of Oklahoma, a tribe with 300,000 members.

My wife can lay claim to a Native American heritage. Her grandmother was part-Cherokee, and her father was born in Tahlequah. Linda had not visited there since she was a little girl, so I suggested in 2014 that we take a road trip to this family homestead.

It turned out to be a colorful excursion that included the discovery of the national coon dog cemetery described in a previous chapter. On the way, we also stopped to visit the Crystal Bridges Museum of American Art in Bentonville, Arkansas. I highly commend it as an exquisite example of what God might have built and the exhibits she might have installed if she had as much money as Alice Walton.

When we planned the trip, I envisioned it as a kind of pilgrimage. However—and I don't mean to be unkind—the town of Tahlequah is a remarkably undistinguished place. Its appearance certainly pales in comparison with Cherokee, North Carolina, the capital of the Eastern Band of Cherokee Indians. (They are the thirteen-thousand-plus descendants of the Native Americans who hid in the Southern Appalachian Mountains when Andrew Jackson's soldiers showed up to arrest them). There, the multi-storied Harrah's Cherokee Casino Resort boasts of 150,000 square feet of gaming, and sparkles with garish neon lighting. Proceeds from the casino help to fund the significantly endowed Cherokee Preservation Foundation that supports economic development, education, cultural preservation, and environmental protection.

By contrast, the Tahlequah gambling hall is a weather-beaten, wood-frame building that could easily be mistaken for a farm implements warehouse. Casino proceeds, such as they are, go to the Cherokee Nation Foundation to support a limited number of scholarships for young people in the tribal area.

Linda's grandmother, Belle Cunningham, was a graduate of the Cherokee National Female Seminary, founded in 1851. The original building of that institution still stands on the campus of what now is Northeastern Oklahoma State University. Linda's grandfather, Thomas Oscar Graham, after completing eighth grade (the highest available schooling) in Charlotte, North Carolina, set out for Oklahoma to seek his fortune. After marrying Belle, he and his wife did indeed prosper and wound up owning a dairy farm, helped establish a bank, and became leading citizens in the community. Regularly, though, he would make the nearly thousand-mile trip by car back to North Carolina to stay in touch with his family and to acquaint himself with new dairy farming techniques and changes in commercial practices.

Now for some brief name-dropping: his young nephew, Billy Franklin Graham, came to Tahlequah from Charlotte in the summers to work on the farm. Yes, I'm referring to the internationally renowned evangelist. In other words, Linda's daddy was Billy Frank's first cousin—a fact of life that the Charlotte family members (all staunch Presbyterians) were discouraged from discussing publicly— so I will not indulge in further gossip.[52]

---

52 Well, all right—maybe just one story. Linda's father, Archie (Billy's cousin), went to the University of Oklahoma, majored in music, and was the drum major of the Sooners' marching band. He came east to Charlotte where he met and courted Linda's mother. Billy was a groomsman in their wedding. In later years, after service abroad during World War II, Archie became a Presbyterian minister. His professional life intersected with Billy Frank (as the family called him) only once. When Billy Frank was asked to conduct a funeral service—a pastoral function he

We spent several hours at the Cherokee National Museum and Cherokee Heritage Center and used the genealogical records of the Cherokee Family Research Center to identify an ancestor from Georgia who may have been forced to relocate to Oklahoma territory. We also found the large farmhouse of her grandfather's dairy. All in all, though, the pilgrimage to the capital of Linda's people was not an especially inspirational journey.

For those who might choose to follow in our tracks anyway, consider a visit to one of the town's biggest attractions. It is a popular restaurant at which we dined one evening: Sam and Ella's Chicken Palace. Its large dining room is filled with porcelain figures of poultry and other chicken-related knickknacks. Yet, for reasons that no one could explain to our satisfaction, this eating spot's specialty is pizza. In fact, I don't think the menu included a reference to any kind of fowl. And so it goes. Not everything is as it appears.

It seems unlikely that we will be paying another visit to Tahlequah in the near future.

---

had never performed—he had to call upon Archie to instruct and assist him.

Three Chords and the Truth

Obviously, any book about the South must include at least a passing reference to country music. Let's face it: country music *is* Southern music. That's why the Grand Old Opry is in Tennessee and not North Dakota. Furthermore, country music sprang from the African American blues, Negro spirituals, and white gospel—all regional sources.

It took a while to acquire my taste for it. The Armed Forces Radio Network in Germany played a lot of what people called "hillbilly" numbers during the year I was an exchange student in Nürnberg, and I was unimpressed. However, during two of my college years, a roommate introduced me to bluegrass music. Dick Stowe taught me the words to "Wildwood Flower" and how to harmonize with him when he sang and fingered his D-18 and D-28 Martin acoustic guitars. After we parted company, though, no one else I knew had ever heard of Ralph Stanley and Bill Monroe, let alone Mike Seeger and the New Lost City Ramblers.[53]

But then I began driving through the South—a region where it often is impossible to find a station on the car radio that doesn't play country music. It didn't take long before I was singing along with the Possum and Willie and Loretta and the rest. And I came to discover that if one is in a receptive frame of mind (going through a divorce, for instance, or coping with the death of a loved one), there is ab-

---

53 I think it was a Garrison Keillor column in which I read that bluegrass derives from plaintive and indeed morbid old Scottish ballads like "The Fatal Wedding." ("The bride, she died at the altar / The bridegroom died next day / The parson dropped dead in the churchyard / as he was about to pray.") Keillor reported having been told that "if someone ain't dead by the third verse, it ain't bluegrass."

solutely nothing that can flat-out bring tears to the eyes like Patsy Cline singing "Crazy" or Kris Kristofferson's scorched voice performing "For the Good Times." Harlan Howard got it right when he described country music as "three chords and the truth."

I hope it won't be too much longer before we visit Nashville again and perhaps get tickets for the Opry. Even if we're successful, though, it won't be as mystical an experience as the Saturday morning during Linda's and my "courtin'" period, when we literally wandered into Ryman Auditorium.

It was a sunny Saturday morning and we had left the hotel to stroll around the old downtown area. Following no prescribed route, we found ourselves beside the battered old Ryman. We literally stepped up from the sidewalk and walked through an open side door. The old building was deserted and very quiet. Nobody challenged our presence, and we could hear our own footsteps as we slowly wandered about. Our voices softened to whispers in this former gospel tabernacle and shrine of country music. The backstage area was littered with debris—music stands, rickety wooden chairs, an old piano. The pews on the main level and the balcony of the auditorium were cracked and scarred. Sunlight streaming through the arched windows outlined thick ribbons of dust motes. The Grand Old Opry had stopped its performances there nearly twenty years earlier, but the ghostly presence of past artists was palpable: Eddy and Roy and Minnie and Hank and Patsy and hundreds more. We were standing on hallowed ground.

Naughty, but Hard to Forget

One of the branches of country music that I enjoy in small batches consists of numbers that are a bit naughty, ornery, or just plain raunchy. Women as well as men have recorded them. I still remember that sweet, innocent-looking, petite, blonde Barbara Mandrell performing "If Loving You Is Wrong, I Don't Want to Be Right."

Earlier I mentioned a friend from Southern California who is better known to himself and even elsewhere as "America's favorite Jewish cowboy minister." (He's the same one who got himself ordained by the Universal Life Church and convinced me to do the same.) Before adopting his clerical vocation, Lon compiled and regularly updated a catalog of uniquely audacious and singularly outrageous Country & Western song titles and lines. Folks from all over the country contributed to the collection.

Here are a few sample lyrics that are difficult to forget:

- "If the phone don't ring, you'll know it's me."
- "I've missed you, but my aim's improvin'."
- "I'm so miserable without you, it's like you're still here."
- "My wife ran off with my best friend, and I miss him."
- "She took my ring and gave me the finger."
- "She's lookin' better with every beer."
- "It's hard to kiss the lips at night that chewed my ass all day."

These lyrics and many others can be crude and often downright misogynistic. But they also—and even simultaneously—can be marked by both poignancy and wit. Having read a draft of this manuscript, some friends have insisted that I add a line from one of their favorite numbers. Written by Waylon Jennings and popularized by Ray Stevens, its memorable refrain is, "Get your tongue out of my mouth, I'm kissing you goodbye."

Christmas on the Riviera

One Christmas, the "kids" were not coming home, and we weren't in the mood for the lengthy travel required to visit them. Staying by ourselves for the holiday didn't seem especially attractive either, so Linda began exploring other options. Her research uncovered a reasonably priced condo on the beach near Panama City—a popular summer resort on a stretch of sand along what folks in these parts call the Redneck Riviera.

We attended a Christmas Eve service in Atlanta and set off the next morning. It was gray and cloudy, but traffic was light. Somewhere below Columbus we crossed into Alabama, stopped for lunch, and then continued to our destination. We had made no plans for dinner but reassured ourselves on the way down that we could always find an American Christmas dinner standby—a Chinese restaurant.

However, once we arrived at our destination, neither the desk clerk nor repeated telephone calls could identify a nearby dining place with an Asian-sounding name or menu. All other restaurants in the vicinity were closed. I knew better than to suggest my preference. Linda had laid down the law soon after we were married: only one Waffle House stop per day, and I had already enjoyed my ration of eggs, smothered hash browns, and patty sausage at noontime.

The sun had set, and now we were getting hungry. Finally, in desperation, we descended to the ground floor, ran across the highway in front of our building, and began to organize a meal from the ingredients offered at a dingy stop-and-shop emporium. We filled a couple of bags with screw-top bottles of wine, packages of cheese crackers, nachos, dip, spicy sausage sticks, and similar fare. I would not describe our holiday repast as delicious, but it did stave off hunger until the next day.

The rest of our holiday was decidedly lacking in festive atmosphere. Linda went for daily walks along the windy beach. I chose to hole up indoors, where I addressed envelopes and added notes for Christmas cards that had not yet been sent. During our stay, a crowd of sadly deluded (or perhaps crazy) Canadians checked in and spent their time outdoors wearing bathing suits in the cold December air, playing on the beach, and romping in the mild Gulf surf. I don't recall seeing the sun for more than a few hours all week. Then it was time to declare the holiday at an end.

We later described to our children the dismal way we had celebrated the holiday—gently implying that it was because they had chosen not to visit us. This parental ploy to evoke feelings of guilt failed to move them to tears. We could imagine them rolling their eyes as they responded by simply wishing us a happy new year.

We have it on good authority that the Gulf Coast region is a delightful destination—in the summer.

Mississippi Meanderings

Too many Southern cities are carbon copies of other metropolises around the country, and our suburban sprawl continues unchecked. That's why it was a special treat when our dear friends, Tom and Jane, volunteered to guide us on a four-day tour of the non-homogenized Mississippi Delta. We didn't go by the Tallahatchie Bridge from which Billy Joe McAllister is reported to have jumped,[54] but we saw plenty to prompt further pondering and reflection.

Our "tour guides" met us, and our journey began by the huge marble fountain in the lobby of Memphis's Peabody Hotel.[55] Each day, to the accompaniment of recorded martial music, a gaggle of mallards, led by a "duck master," resplendent in a red uniform and hat, steps off an elevator and marches to that fountain. They jump in and paddle about until later afternoon when they return in similar celebratory fashion to their home on the roof of the building.

A plaque on the outside of the hotel proclaims: "The Mississippi Delta begins in the lobby of the Peabody Hotel and ends on Catfish Row in Vicksburg. . . . If you stand in the middle of the lobby, where the ducks waddle and turtles drowse, you will see everybody who is anybody in the Delta." From further research I learned that although the plaque expresses some color-

---

54 "Ode to Billy Joe," composed and recorded by Bobbie Gentry in 1967.

55 Most visitors are unaware that the hotel was named to honor George Peabody, whose generosity to Southern education after the Civil War helped to set in motion a reclamation of the devastated region.

ful and quotable sentiment, much of its text is private conjecture and prone to error.[56]

Crossing the state line into Mississippi, we entered DeSoto County and passed through Hernando, its principal town. Those names are important reminders about another often-neglected part of Southern history—the extensive exploration of the region by the Spanish long before the arrival of the first English and other European settlers.

Our first stop was the University of Mississippi (the site of virulent resistance when James Meredith sought admission in 1964). A visit to Oxford also necessitated a pilgrimage to William Faulkner's home at Rowan Oak, and a stop at Square Books on the town square. There I purchased the print of a photograph that captures Elvis Presley extolling the virtues of literacy.

We next headed west, traveling back roads through desolately beautiful fields almost devoid of people and empty of most structures except churches. We passed through Marks[57] and continued to Jonestown. There, a valiant band of Catholic nuns had spent two decades establishing a Montessori school, an after-school tutoring center, parenting classes, and a clinic–the only locally available health care in this small, desperately poor town.[58]

---

56 The citation is taken from *God Shakes Creation* (New York: Harper & Brothers, 1936), written by David Cohn, the journalist son of a Polish Jew who immigrated to Mississippi.

57 Here, over the years, the Quitman County Development Association has worked to build an African American credit union that is helping to create place-based capital.

58 A year after our visit to Jonestown, Charles Simic, the Serbian American, Pulitzer Prize-winning poet and U.S., poet laureate, described it thusly: "There are towns like Jonestown, Mississippi, that in their shocking poverty make one gasp. Weathered, sagging and unpainted houses, boarded-up windows, others covered with plastic, yards full of dismantled rusty cars, their parts scattered about amid all kinds of other junk and trash, are everywhere. Idle people of all ages lounge on collapsing porches or stand on street corners waiting for something to do. In the countryside with its fertile dark soil, soybeans have become the chief crop, poultry farms are a major business, and there are nine gambling casinos in the next county. All that has increased per capita income in the region, but there was no evidence of it among the Blacks I saw." Charles Simic, *Memory Piano*, (Ann Arbor: The University of Michigan Press, 2006).

That first evening of what had been a long day, we enjoyed catfish, hush puppies, and fried green tomatoes and listened to live blues musicians at Morgan Freeman's Ground Zero, in Clarksville. We spent the night at the Shack-Up Inn, a funky "Bed and Beer" hostelry formed by the assemblage of a converted cotton gin and a collection of shacks and silos. Our room was in one of the silos, and the bed had a chenille spread that was complemented by a pillow on which rested a Moon Pie—all self-consciously kitschy but enjoyable, nonetheless.

Other sights and sounds as we continued our travels: breakfast in a diner owned by a Lebanese family whose framed family tree in Arabic hung on the wall; an unmarked restaurant in Marigold whose gardens wrapped around a pottery studio; the town of Greenwood transformed by the arrival of Viking Ranges;[59] driving past Parchman Farm, the notorious prison. . . .

We spent the night in the lodge on a wilderness preserve that was teeming with migratory birds and deer and was located beside an oxbow lake created in ages past, when the Mississippi River decided to change direction. The next morning, headed toward Vicksburg, we came upon Margaret's Grocery and Bible Café. Distinguished by its red, white, and blue towers and arches, it offers thousands of hand-lettered, biblically based injunctions—including this one from Margaret's preacher husband who built the entire complex: "You can do right if you want to."

After solemnly touring the Union and Confederate monuments on the battlefields overlooking Vicksburg, we visited the establishment where Coca-Cola was first bottled, drifted south to Port Gibson (General Grant said it was too lovely to burn) and saw another example of the effort to preserve old Jewish synagogues across the rural South.

Near sundown, we navigated a dirt road to the ruins of the Windsor, a once palatial antebellum home, its massive Corinthian

---

59 The city fell on hard times again after the sale of the company, although the elegant Alluvian Hotel still stands.

columns standing silently among the pines. (Later we observed some of the elaborate wrought iron work taken from the Windsor and now adorning the front of the chapel at historically Black Alcorn State University.)

We stopped to see a portion of the original Natchez Trace, worn deep into the earth from the hordes who traversed it, and then drove into Natchez itself for our last night's lodging in a beautifully restored plantation house. One could imagine it before the Civil War, when two-thirds of America's millionaires are reputed to have lived between Natchez and New Orleans. In contrast, one year after Appomattox, a large portion of Mississippi's budget went to purchase artificial limbs for veterans of the war.

The next morning, we toured Longwood, an unfinished, six-story, thirty-two-room, octagonal mansion. Work on it had stopped in April 1861 when the Philadelphia workmen dropped their saws and hammers after war was declared and fled north. And then it was on to New Orleans, the Carousel Bar at the Monteleone Hotel, and the end of our Mississippi sojourn.

We had seen wealth and grinding poverty. Our trip had taken us through the worst sections of towns that are losing population. We also had visited communities that may be coming back to life. Prisons and casinos represent economic hope for some places, while others have turned to eco-tourism, new forms of agriculture, and other creative approaches to survival. Don't try to explain it; just absorb it. Like other parts of the South, Mississippi draws much of its soul and sense of itself from a rich mixture of paradox and eccentricity.

The City That Care Forgot

Many wonderful writers have penned their own paeans to New Orleans—otherwise known as the Big Easy, the Crescent City, NOLA, N'Awlins, N'erlins. Perhaps my all-time favorite description came from Tom Robbins:

> Louisiana in September was like an obscene phone call from nature. The air—moist, sultry, secretive, and far from fresh—felt as if it were being exhaled into one's face. Sometimes it even sounded like heavy breathing. Honeysuckle, swamp flowers, magnolia, and the mystery smell of the river scented the atmosphere, amplifying the intrusion of organic sleaze. It was aphrodisiac and repressive, soft and violent at the same time. In New Orleans, in the French Quarter, miles from the barking lungs of alligators, the air maintained this quality of breath, although here it acquired a tinge of metallic halitosis, due to fumes expelled by tourist buses, trucks delivering Dixie beer, and, on Decatur Street, a mass-transit motor coach named Desire.[60]

Other Southern cities have charm, atmosphere, and colorful ambience, but, so far as I am concerned, New Orleans is the only one to which the term "exotic" can accurately be applied.

---

60 Tom Robbins, *Jitterbug Perfume* (New York: Bantam Books, 1984).

I have visited the city so many times that the images all blur . . . but what wonderful images: fog rolling off the Mississippi River late at night and twisting itself around the street lights in Jackson Square, as a lone blues musician on a bench picks at a guitar; other sounds of music pouring out the windows of Preservation Hall and less famous jazz joints; the sound of horses' hooves clip-clopping their way through the streets and past the ironwork balconies and fences of the French Quarter; the scent of fresh coffee brewing at dawn in the market on Decatur Street, almost strong enough to erase the stench of spilled stale beer from the night before.

It is impossible to engage in a discussion about New Orleans without introducing the topic of food. I can't think of any other place in the United States where the local culture is as dominated by the subjects of eating and drinking as in New Orleans. I still recall an evening at Arnaud's, seated at a table with local board members from Xavier University. These women and men were educators and businesspeople whose careers had nothing to do with the culinary arts. Yet, to my astonishment, they were able to carry on an intense ten-minute conversation in which the only issue debated was the merit of putting okra into gumbo.

Helping Xavier University to launch the first capital campaign in its history meant frequent visits to New Orleans. Clarence Jupiter, Xavier's chief development officer, enjoyed introducing me to a wide range of restaurants, many owned by African Americans, that I never would have found if I had depended upon white guidebooks. At the top of the list by virtue of its menu and ambience was Dooky Chase's. It stands on Orleans Avenue, across the street from a large public housing project. Named for Edgar "Dooky" Chase, Jr., a former band leader and entrepreneur, it was presided over by his widow, the elegant Leah Chase, the "Queen of Creole Cooking."[61] For politicians, business leaders, entertainers, and other celebrities, it was a regular

---

61 Mrs. Chase died in 2019.

stop. The main dining room, which featured a wide variety of culinary specials, also functioned as a gallery of original African American art.

On my first visit to New Orleans, Curtis Dixon[62] took me to Antoine's for dinner. The *pompano en papillote* and the rest of the exquisite meal carried my taste buds to new heights, and my stroll down Bourbon Street after our meal stimulated other senses. I had been to the Playboy Club in Manhattan and had visited a few go-go establishments, but never had I been in such proximity to that much quivering, naked, female flesh. Small wonder that the gustatory and visual treasures of this remarkable city—all displayed against the backdrop of throbbing music—captured what continues to be my undying appreciation.

It is difficult to get a bad meal in the Crescent City. One example of that axiom which occurs to me involves a late Saturday morning many years later. Linda and I were wandering down Decatur Street when it began to rain. Confronted with the decision of whether to buy an umbrella or a drink, we slipped into a small, dark, grimy hole-in-the-wall that reeked of stale beer and found a table. The bar stools were occupied by a ramshackle group of men who looked as if they had been there since eight o'clock—whether that morning or the night before wasn't clear.

As we sipped our large Bloody Marys, and the rain continued to pour down outside, we noticed that other patrons were ordering steaming bowls of gumbo. The room was fortunately too dark to permit a sanitation audit, so we took a chance and

---

62 J. Curtis Dixon merits a full-length biography. His career began as a small-town teacher in rural Georgia, from which he progressed to become a principal, county school superintendent, state superintendent of school administration and finance, and State Agent for Negro Schools. He earned his doctorate in education from Teachers College of Columbia University, became a board member of the Rosenwald Fund and the General Education Board, Vice Chancellor of the University of Georgia, Vice President of Mercer University, and then President of the Southern Education Foundation. I once asked him how he came to spend a career promoting the education of African Americans. A humble spirit, he declined to elaborate, saying simply that the segregated patterns of education he first encountered as a teacher and principal "just didn't seem right."

ordered some for ourselves. It was as fine a concoction as I've ever sent down my throat: dark as the Mississippi River where it passes Baton Rouge (that's an old Justin Wilson[63] saying), with a heady combination of seafood, chicken, and sausage heaped upon a mound of white rice! As another saying in these parts goes, it was so good that it made you want to "slap yo' momma." We washed down our final swallows of the gumbo with another pair of Bloody Marys. Then—the rain having stopped—we walked the three blocks to our room at the guesthouse on Esplanade, collapsed on the bed, and took an early nap.

---

63 Famed television cooking show host whose specialty was Cajun dishes.

Travels with Andy

Over the years, as I traveled around the South and other parts of the country, I have periodically had interesting traveling companions.

There was the time that Lou Holtz, then still the head coach of the University of Arkansas football team and a gifted comedian, kept a group of us entertained with a humorous, non-stop monologue on an afternoon flight from Little Rock to Dallas.

On another occasion, I wound up in the deserted Delta Crown Room at the Columbia, South Carolina, airport with Frank McGuire, the legendary basketball coach. Older readers may remember that he was the man who changed the game of round ball in the South by importing players from New York high schools. If only I had had a tape recorder to capture his colorful stories about his days at the University of North Carolina and later directing the play of Wilt Chamberlain and the other Philadelphia Warriors . . . not to mention the observations about his own "crazy" protégé, Al McGuire (no relation), another famous basketball coach!

The company may have been less informative, but another time I really did board a small plane in Bloomington, Indiana and flew to Urbana, Illinois, accompanied only by crates of guinea pigs, stacked three-high on the other seats in the cabin. As best I was able to determine, it was also a business trip for them, going from one university laboratory to another.

Not all of my seatmates were small animals or athletic personalities. Another story to be told someday involves a flight from Atlanta to Mobile on which I was seated next to the author, John Updike.

Two of the most interesting encounters, though, were with Andrew Young, pastor, civil rights leader, former U.S. Representative from the Fifth District of Georgia, former Mayor of Atlanta, former U.S. Ambassador to the United Nations, and neighbor. Andy (as everyone in Atlanta calls him) and I have a rather curious relationship. We have been together on numerous occasions, so I'm reasonably sure he recognizes my face; however, if we have been formally introduced (and it's possible that we never were), I don't think he knows my name. During his first run for a seat in the U.S. House of Representatives, we held a fundraiser for him in our home. However, Andy, then the head of the Atlanta Human Relations Commission, was trying to negotiate a strike settlement at a local Mead Paper plant, so he couldn't be there. His gracious wife, Jean, filled in for him.

He and I were first together on a platform for administrators and other dignitaries when he spoke at a Clark College commencement; I later recruited him to speak at a seminar that Clark sponsored in Chicago; and he also delivered a eulogy for Vivian Henderson, the President of Clark College.

Sometime thereafter, I flew to New Orleans late one afternoon for an evening banquet at which Dr. Henderson was to be posthumously honored. Andy was also there to speak at the banquet. (New Orleans, by the way, is Andy's hometown.)

Because I had business in Atlanta the next day, I had booked a return flight that left at 2 a.m. I hung around the lobby for several hours after the ceremonies, talking with Bayard Rustin and several of his associates before taking a cab to the airport. When I boarded the Delta plane, I found myself seated next to Andy. No sooner were we airborne than he turned to me and proceeded to expound for the entire one-hour flight—I'm serious!—about why Jimmy Carter should be the next President of the United States. If I remember correctly, a key part of his case was that Carter understood Black Americans and knew more of them than any of the other white candidates. Andy never asked for my name or called me by it.

The rest of the story, of course, is that with the help of Andy

Young and many other members of the Peanut Brigade, Carter became the 39th U.S. President.

Time passed, and then it was time for another presidential election season (in 2000, as I recall). I was sitting in the main terminal at Dulles Airport, waiting to board the "People Mover" that would shuttle me to my Atlanta-bound plane. Andy appeared and sat down beside me. Without a word of introduction and after only the briefest of pauses, Andy launched into a lengthy and cogent soliloquy about why General Colin Powell should/could be the next U.S. President. One of his points was that Powell ought to be able to mobilize the votes of virtually all military servicepeople and veterans, regardless of their skin color. That was our last encounter, although Andy was later a speaker at a couple of the Southeastern Council of Foundations' annual conferences while I was involved with that organization.

Andy no longer lives in my neighborhood, so there are fewer opportunities to bump into him and smile and wave at the pharmacy or dry cleaner. That noted, though, recently Linda spotted him renewing his car registration at the motor vehicles office and greeted him with a "Good morning, Mr. Ambassador." He smiled back, but he doesn't know her name either.

Part Four
THIS LAND IS OUR LAND

Another New South

A friend who recently attended an academic colloquium in one of those decaying "Rust Belt" cities up North still hasn't stopped gushing about the sheer "ethnicity" of the place. I know exactly what he means. One of the features I used to miss most about my former region of residence was its cultural and linguistic diversity.

There's an old cartoon whose humor may be lost on many Southerners. It shows an ophthalmologist pointing to one of the lower lines on an eye chart—a jumble of letters, mostly consonants—and looking quizzically at his frowning patient. The patient's response is the cartoon's caption: "I'm not sure I can pronounce it, but I think he played left tackle for Notre Dame."

Let me illustrate my point in another way. For seven years in the 1970s and 80s, *Barney Miller* was a popular situation comedy series about police detectives in their squad room on the east side of Greenwich Village in New York City. Played by Hal Linden, Capt. Barney Miller was surrounded by a colorful assortment of other cops. The characters included Stan Wojciehowicz, a Polish American Roman Catholic; Ron Harris, a dilettantish African American author; Nick Yamada, a taciturn Japanese American; Arthur Dietrich, who seemed to be Jewish; and Miguel "Chano" Amenguale, a Puerto Rican. (It was never stated, but I assume that Abe Vigoda, who played the grumpy Phil Fish, was intended to be Italian.) Clearly the series could never have been staged in a Southern setting. Where, with the possible exception of New Orleans, could one assemble that much ethnic and racial variety and still have it seem thoroughly natural?

During the time I was a reporter in the steel town of Youngstown, Ohio, the city had its own Ukrainian, Yugoslavian, Croatian,

Romanian, German, Italian, and Irish neighborhoods, and they all had their own clubs and bars, Roman Catholic parishes, funeral homes, and restaurants. There also was a residentially segregated African American district. The whole picture underscored the concept of "melting pot," and, lest it be forgotten, one of the major crucibles—at least for white immigrants—was the public-school system.

During the early years of white settlement, the South absorbed a goodly share of Northern Irish and Scots as well as Germans. Then in the period before the Civil War, European immigration to the region essentially slowed to a trickle. Certainly, it never approached the size of the colorful tidal wave of newcomers who poured into Northern and Midwestern cities. The South essentially locked itself into a white-and-Black dynamic—one segment free, the other mostly enslaved or persecuted. The WASPs (White Anglo Saxon Protestants) further extended their attitude of racial and ethnic superiority to other kinds of immigrants; Catholics and Jews were not especially welcome.

But the newcomers persisted. Eventually, a typical Southern community evolved to have a Greek restaurant, a Chinese laundry, a Jewish dry goods store, and a pizzeria owned and operated by immigrant families. Missing, though, was the dense potpourri of menus, accents, and music so common elsewhere in the country. There, a customer entering a Czech-owned bakery placed her order in a Slovakian dialect; the butcher posted his specials in Polish. These small businesses offered a comforting and nostalgic reminder of old times and cultures. Much as I came to love the South, I did miss the way in which one's daily life elsewhere in the country was often enhanced and enriched by being wrapped in the patchwork quilt of global variety.[64]

---

64 Another usually overlooked chapter of Southern history is the immigration of Chinese to the region after having been lured by the gold rush in the West and the construction of the trans-continental railroad. Many Chinese migrants came South immediately after the Civil War when laborers were needed for the plantations that had previously been tended by enslaved people. It continued until 1882 and the passage of the Chinese Exclusion Act. The largest numbers settled in the Mississippi Delta where many eventually became shopkeepers serving Black communities. New Orleans for a time had a significant Chinatown. These Asian newcomers also found their way to other portions of the South: for example, Greenwood Cemetery in Atlanta, less than a mile from my house, has an entire section of Chinese graves.

But change is on the way. The South is finally experiencing its own new immigration era. Large numbers of both legal and illegal individuals and families are arriving from Latin America, Asia, Africa, and, to some extent, the Middle East. Because they are not only migrant farm workers, hidden from view in the region's fields, it is becoming increasingly difficult for people who disapprove to ignore their presence.

For example, it is possible to spend a long time in the Buford Corridor, an eight-mile stretch of State Road 13 on the northside of Atlanta, without hearing a word of or reading a sign in English. This epicenter of Latino and Asian commerce is home to about one thousand ethnically diverse businesses and retail establishments.

Other evidence abounds. The dominance of football as the regional religion is being undercut by the popularity of soccer. Hindu temples and Muslim mosques are appearing in many metropolitan areas. Tiny Clarkston, Georgia, on the outskirts of Atlanta (7,500 people living within a square mile) is home to immigrants from every part of the world. Students in the high school come from about fifty different countries.

The new immigrants have faced and will continue to face hostility and discrimination. Sad to note, those with darker skin tones will be targeted for abuse by the South's still-plentiful supply of racists. They may be hampered by language barriers and limited financial resources. But over time, like the newcomers who preceded them, some will be grudgingly welcomed because they can offer the cheap labor that makes it possible for the rest of us to maintain our middle-class lifestyle. Many of them, though, will persevere and even prosper as they find employment, save money, send their children to school, purchase residences, start their own businesses, and even get elected to political office.

Yet another New South may be on the horizon.

Learning Our Colors

Back in the 1950s, those of us white folks raised in liberal circles were taught to treat African Americans with "tolerance." It was intended to be an alternative to the bigotry and discrimination that abounded—and I guess it was. Instead of challenging the ugly clichés about Black people, this way of thinking affirmed that their "failings" were no reason to hate them. After all, it wasn't their fault that they were "different."

Time passed, new laws were enacted, attitudes changed, and the next thing we knew, an acceptable and even preferred approach was for us to declare ourselves to be color-blind. In our defense, this new affirmation was honestly intended to be a heartfelt denial of racial prejudice—kind of a secular derivative of those lines from the old Sunday School hymn: "Jesus loves the little children / All the children of the world / Red and yellow, Black and white / They are precious in his sight / Jesus loves the little children of the world."

Even at a young age, though, I sensed that this simplistic theological abstraction didn't fully describe the true situation. Whatever Jesus may have thought about the world's little children, the world seemed to be giving most Black people the short end of the stick.

One of the great gifts that accompanied my four years of travel through the South and the move to Clark College and Southwest Atlanta was that I became intensely color conscious. It became impossible to enter a room without instinctively conducting a quick visual census of African Americans and Caucasians. If we went to a classical concert, I immediately conducted a mental poll of "Black" faces in the orchestra or chorus. I kept careful score of African

Americans in attendance at conferences. Conversely, as often the only white person on the scene, I gained a new appreciation of what it felt like to "stand out."

Color-blind? No way. An African American friend put it this way: "I don't trust people who say they don't see skin color unless they are legally blind."

Another piece of racial myth that was exposed as patent non-sense was the familiar white platitude: "All Black people look the same to me." Anyone who can't tell the difference between Denzel Washington and Ving Rhames (remember the gangster Marcellus in *Pulp Fiction*?) is either a liar or a fool . . . or in need of a good ophthalmologist.

At any rate, it didn't take long during my immersion into life at Clark College before I also began to have a heightened appreciation for the nuances of pigmentation. My new friends and colleagues and neighbors came in a wide range of skin tones. Picking up my cues from them, I learned to describe African Americans with terms like "dark-skinned," "brown," "light-skinned," and, yes, "Black."

Along the way I discovered a kind of literary parallel to the color-blindness error. When some white Southerner authors write about their region (indeed when most white Americans write about their country), they all too easily slip into generalizations that completely ignore the past or present existence of African Americans and other so-called ethnic minorities. I certainly have been guilty of this transgression in the past but have tried hard not to repeat it in this book.

It's a bad habit that is easily acquired and difficult to discard. After all, for the better part of four centuries, we white folks have described our past and our current affairs as if "people of color" failed to exist. A pronouncement that begins, "In the South, we . . ." or "Southerners have always . . ." should sound an immediate alarm bell and call us to question its complete validity. One can test my proposition by pulling off the shelf almost any book by a white author that purports to describe life in the South or, for that matter, life anywhere in the United States, reading a descriptive paragraph and then questioning whether it applies to or acknowledges equally the existence of all Americans.

I don't know how long it will take for us, as they say in kindergarten, to learn our colors, but time's a-wastin'.

Giving Credit Where
Credit Is Due

A word of warning. The following piece is going to wander a bit, but, as I have come to learn, that's the way of storytelling in the South.

When I was a small boy, we did a lot of singing in elementary school. One of the songs that we would lustily belt out was about the boll weevil who was "just a-lookin' for a home." Way up there in New Jersey, the song simply had a catchy tune. We didn't have a clue about the meaning of what once had been an old blues number created by an African American guitar-picker in Mississippi. Never having seen a cotton plant, we didn't realize that the hungry Black bug being "celebrated" in song was a villain. This dreaded insect had invaded our country toward the end of the nineteenth century and come close to destroying the entire cotton-growing industry of the South by the 1920s.

That's a round-about way to lead into the real point I want to make—and I'm not there yet.

To continue . . . down in Enterprise, Alabama, there's a statue on the town square to celebrate that same boll weevil, the scourge of cotton-growing farmers in Coffee County and the rest of the South. Why? Well, according to the accounts I've read, as farmers were watching their main cash crop being destroyed, a fellow named H. M. Sessions showed up. He convinced one of those farmers, C. W. Baston, to convert his property to fields of peanut plants. Baston did, and he prospered. Other growers also diversified their crops, and the entire area did well economically. Bon Fleming, a local businessman, came up with the idea to build a statue to honor the pest that had been a catalyst for positive change. It went up in 1919. The statue (or at least a replica of the original) is still standing in the heart of town.

The first time I heard that story, I was impressed by the clear sense of whimsy and irony that Mr. Fleming possessed, and I will continue to honor him for his inventiveness.

However, another question has been nagging me. Who came up with the idea of using peanuts to replace cotton as a profitable commodity? Maybe they didn't teach the answer to that question in the South, but up North we learned that a Negro professor at a school in Alabama was one of the first to recommend alternative crops to counter soil depletion. He also invented so many uses for peanuts that it made perfect sense to grow lots of them.

So, where's the statue that honors this hero, George Washington Carver?

Understandably, there's a bust of him at Tuskegee University (then Tuskegee Institute) where he taught and did his research, and there's a likeness of him as a young boy at the George Washington Carver National Monument near his birthplace in Missouri.[65]

But . . .

Here, at last, is my point: isn't it about time for the farmers' associations of the South to raise the needed funds and establish a fitting memorial to the man who almost single-handedly saved their daddies' and granddaddies' butts, as some Southerners might say, and laid the foundation for a new era of prosperous Southern agriculture? It doesn't have to be a statue; how about a significant endowment gift to Tuskegee University!

Come to think of it, though, perhaps we should launch a new season of statue-shaping to honor African American Southerners who brought about positive change to the region. Villa Rica, Georgia, has a statue of Thomas A. Dorsey, the "father of gospel

---

65 Established in 1943 by Franklin Delano Roosevelt; the first national monument dedicated to a Black American and the first to a non-president.

music," and Ruleville, Mississippi, has a larger-than-life likeness of Fannie Lou Hamer, the civil rights heroine. But there is room for many more African American heroes. Apparently, the Andrew W. Mellon Foundation agrees. I read recently that it has earmarked $250 million for the re-telling of history in public space through the commissioning of "alternative" statues.

Robert E. Lee Has
Left the Building

On the morning of December 21, 2020, a small crew of workers removed the life-sized statue of Robert E. Lee from its pedestal in the National Statuary Hall of the U.S. Capitol. As approved by the Virginia General Assembly, the homage to General Lee will be replaced by a likeness of Barbara Rose Johns. She is the remarkable Black teenager who, in 1951, led a protest against the racial segregation of her high school in Farmville, Virginia, and thereby launched an epic civil rights battle in Prince Edward County. Her figure will stand beside that of another Virginian—George Washington. The removal of "Marse Robert" was yet another step in a series of actions to obliterate the hundreds of tributes to Lee and other Confederate leaders from public places throughout the South.

When I first came to the South, Richmond, Virginia, set the standard for Southern reverence toward its Civil War leaders. Nowhere was the hero worship more pronounced than in the capital of the Confederacy. The most dominating demonstration of that sentiment was along Monument Avenue, a high-tone residential boulevard in the "Fan" district. That celebration of military valor and/or white supremacy (depending upon one's perspective) began with the erection of a statue of Robert E. Lee in 1890. It was followed early in the next century by the figures of James Ewell Brown ("Jeb") Stuart, Jefferson Davis, and Thomas Jonathan (Stonewall) Jackson.[66]

---

66 Three of the four (Stuart is not included) also are depicted in the famous relief carving on the side of Stone Mountain in Georgia. Curiously, the Monument

The debate over the propriety of Civil War memorials smoldered for a long time. It took the recent killings of Black men and women by law enforcement officers and white vigilantes to stir the glowing embers into blazing flames. Sometimes assisted by crowds with tools of demolition, tributes to the Confederacy's military warriors began tumbling to the ground. The monuments that escaped destruction are being relocated or put in mothballs until civil authorities can reach decisions about their futures. Today, less than a year after the demolition began, all of Monument Avenue's old statues are gone.

It seems to be worth noting that a quarter-century ago, Richmond's leaders overcame bitter opposition and erected a statue of Arthur Ashe at the far western end of the street. Ashe, a native of the city, was the first Black tennis player selected to the United States Davis Cup team and the only Black man ever to win the singles titles at Wimbledon, the U.S. Open, and the Australian Open. Today, only Ashe's statue remains on Arthur Ashe Boulevard epitomize the pride of Virginia in its native sons.

Another more recent and heretical shift occurred when the Virginia Museum of Fine Arts commissioned a statue by Kehinde Wiley, a young African American artist. *Rumors of War*, inspired (according to the artist) by the Richmond statue of J.E.B. Stuart, depicts a young Black man in a heroic pose, seated upon a muscular horse, but the rider has dreadlocks in a ponytail and wears jeans ripped at the knees and Nike high-top sneakers. After a preview in New York City's Times Square, the statue was moved in 2019 to its permanent location at the entrance to the museum.

Like the Moses of the Old Testament who destroyed the statue of the golden calf in the wilderness, some folks will not be satisfied until all vestiges of Confederate imagery have vanished. Others would be willing to let them stand so long as their presence is explained with some prominently displayed interpretive language.

Avenue array concluded with the statue of a seated Matthew Thomas Maury, a Confederate naval officer who never fought a battle but became renowned as an oceanographer.

I can argue the case either way and leave the controversy to folks whose passions about it are stronger than mine. However, because we know that these monuments exist to undergird an historical untruth and, at least implicitly, to promote white superiority, I contend that permitting them simply to remain as they are is unacceptable.

Before closing, though, I'd like to share a few more musings on the subject:

I would give odds that most Southerners don't know the names of the hundreds of Confederate military veterans still showcased in their capitals and town squares. Until the recent wave of iconoclasm, I would have been hard pressed to identify the fellow on horseback across the street from the church I have attended for almost five decades.[67]

It seems that the reverence for the images of those defenders of slavery and Jim Crow can be more of a knee-jerk reaction than a matter of doctrine. A possible example involves the fist-brandishing statue of Thomas Watson, the populist-turned-segregationist and anti-Catholic and anti-Jewish bigot. A few years ago, not for the first time, a faction of citizens felt it was inappropriate for Mr. Watson's likeness to dominate the front steps the Georgia State Capitol.

Governor Nathan Deal chose not to join the debate. Instead, on a state holiday (ironically, the delayed celebration of Robert E. Lee's birthday that year), when the capitol grounds were largely deserted, he had workmen remove it for later placement in a park across the street. The official reason given had to do with the deteriorating of the steps on which the bronze statue stood. The public outcry, if I missed it, must have been very *sotto voce*.

As promised, the figure did reappear, but it's no longer visible from the street. To find it now, one must first walk into a small park across Washington Street, past the statue of former Governor and Senator Herman Talmadge (who also successfully used racism as a

---

67 By the way, I went over and checked. The horseman is John B. Gordon, one of Robert E. Lee's most trusted generals. He's still there, but the street that was once named for him now bears the name of Ralph David Abernathy, one of Martin Luther King, Jr.'s most trusted "generals."

fuel for political success). However, we no longer hear much about Watson, so maybe there's something to that "out of sight, out of mind" concept.

The Watson story reminds me in turn of the occasion when the Southeastern Council of Foundations had arranged to hold its annual meeting in Biloxi, Mississippi. It was during a period of angry debate about whether the state flag should include the battle pennant of the Confederacy. Several of our members had strong feelings (on both sides) about the subject.

I arrived at the conference site early and wandered into the empty main ballroom. On the corner of the stage stood a Mississippi flag with the disputed design. No one else was around. I climbed onto the stage and moved the flag to a dark backstage corner. It never re-appeared, nor did I receive any requests for its return. And guess what? Even as I was rewriting this chapter, the Mississippi legislature "retired" the state flag and commissioned the design of a new one, and the state university quietly relocated the problematic statue of a Confederate soldier from its prominent location to an out-of-the-way cemetery.

Perhaps Robert E. Lee himself should have the last word on the subject. In 1869, he was invited to help commemorate the Battle of Gettysburg with "enduring memorials of granite." The general declined the invitation for unrelated reasons, but pointedly added, "I think it wiser, moreover, not to keep open the sores of war but to follow the examples of those nations who endeavored to obliterate the marks of civil strife, to commit to oblivion the feelings engendered."[68]

---

68 Accessed 2018, *https://www.pbs.org/newshour/nation/robert-e-lee-opposed -confederate-monuments.*

Times Forgotten

As I hope I've made clear, I love the South, with a special affection for the unique embellishments that highlight its difference from the rest of the country. However, still running through the heart of our region are the strains of a virus that continues to cripple us. It is evident in the claim that old times in the South are not forgotten.

There are Southerners who regard that line from what they consider to be their battle hymn as an expression of reverence for the past. They are mistaken. All too often it is simply a celebration of inaccurate memory. Memory does not need to depend upon facts for its preservation; emotion will suffice to keep it alive and permit it to rise to the level of mythology.

Seemingly within minutes after Robert E. Lee surrendered his sword to Ulysses S. Grant at Appomattox Court House in Virginia in 1865, other Southerners grabbed their pens and began rewriting their region's history. It was the story of what they called the Lost Cause. The myth that it nostalgically propagated was of chivalrous, outnumbered Confederate soldiers defending their benevolent plantation lifestyle against an aggressive and industrially dominated Northern offensive. Its recitation was an emotionally satisfying antidote to the bitterness of defeat.

It didn't take long for the Lost Cause to be enshrined in the region's schoolbooks and otherwise kept fervently alive in the minds of generations of Southerners. This corruption of the facts steadily worked its way into the consciousness of white Americans everywhere.

Not content with fabricating an inaccurate past, some white Southerners next began marketing an expurgated picture of their post-war region to attract badly needed Northern investment. Henry Grady, managing editor of *The Atlanta Constitution*, was among the first of many hustlers to play fast and loose with the truth. Employing skillful rhetoric, he and his fellow promoters proclaimed the existence of a New South that didn't exist, glossing over the almost total disenfranchisement of African Americans that was the order of the day. That pattern of distortion continued for many years.

Indeed, it continues to rear its head. In 2002, the Robert E. Lee Chapter of the Sons of Confederate Veterans erected an obelisk in the town square of Nashville, Georgia. Chiseled on that stone pillar are these words: [69]

> APPROXIMATELY 260,000
> SOUTHERNERS WERE
> KILLED OR WOUNDED
> WHILE DEFENDING
> THE CONSTITUTIONAL
> FREEDOMS WHICH WERE
> HANDED DOWN BY OUR
> FOUNDING FATHERS. ALL
> RACES AND RELIGIONS JOINED
> TOGETHER TO DEFEND THE
> CONFEDERACY, THEIR FAMILIES,
> THEIR PROPERTY, AND
> STATES RIGHTS AGAINST
> NORTHERN AGGRESSION LED
> BY ABRAHAM LINCOLN.

Many of us have been cheated by this manipulation and hiding of the truth since we were young. When I first visited Washington, DC as a boy, nobody told me that slaves were utilized to build the

---

69 Copied from a photograph taken by Laura McCarty, President, Georgia Humanities, 2018.

U.S. Capitol and the White House. My high school teachers neglected to mention that enslaved Black labor in the South played a major role in the building of Northern industrial wealth.

In later years, when I was employed by the Woodrow Wilson National Fellowship Foundation in Princeton, it never occurred to me to question the organization's name. Omitted from mention in the standard biographical information about Woodrow Wilson was his virulent racism that set back the Africa-American gains in federal employment during Reconstruction. [70]

With a handful of notable exceptions, Black achievement received scant mention in the books and articles I read. Scholars like Carter G. Woodson, the African American historian who created Negro History Week[71] in 1926, and his colleagues often were fighting an uphill battle. And sometimes revelation proceeds very slowly. Only this past year did I learn that thirty of the buildings on the beautiful Duke University campus in Durham, North Carolina, were designed by Julian Abele, the first African American graduate from the University of Pennsylvania's school of architecture. Other scholars like Eric Foner, who wrote the seminal book[72] about the post-Civil War years and other historical "exposés," also helped to begin removing the veil that masked the truth of our past.

I believe that the most important challenge facing the South—indeed, the nation—is to vaccinate itself against deceptive and incomplete history by securing and widely publicizing an accurate account of the past. The current search for truth includes the vitally important 1619 Project, created by Nikole Hannah-Jones of *The New York Times.* It also embraces the work of the Equal Justice Initiative, which builds in turn upon the pioneering journalism of Ida B. Wells as it dredges up the ugly history of lynchings. We need

---

70 The foundation recently re-christened itself as The Institute for Citizens and Scholars.

71 It officially evolved into Black History Month when President Gerald Ford called for its nationwide observance in 1976.

72 Eric Foner, *Reconstruction: America's Unfinished Revolution*, 1863-1877 (New York: Harper & Row, 1988).

even more explorations of this kind by academic institutions, government agencies, ecclesiastical bodies, and even families. The results of the research will not always be welcome, but they will help to secure a civil society.

Twelfth Night

It's January 6—the Feast of the Epiphany, Three Kings Day, better known in our home simply as Twelfth Night (as in "On the twelfth day of Christmas, my true love gave to me. . ."). We are preparing for the onslaught of more than one hundred guests of various age, occupation, ethnicity, sexual preference, and hue. It's a jamboree that has been going on for well over a quarter-century. When trying to describe the barely controlled chaos, I have sometimes fallen back on the analogy of the cocktail party in Holly Golightly's apartment in the film version of *Breakfast at Tiffany's*.

Included on the invitation list have been neighbors, professional colleagues, clients, fellow church members, ordained clergy, politicians, foundation executives, and the guy who cuts my hair. During the course of these evenings, guests have announced their bids for public office, shown off their newborn children, and discovered distantly related family members they didn't know existed.

A few words of background explanation. We stumbled upon this date for a celebration when renovations to our kitchen forced the delay of our annual holiday party. It became an immoveable feast, always occurring on January 6, no matter the day of the week on which it falls.

The event has undergone several metamorphoses. What began as a simple gathering for a few people exploded over the years into a party for seventy-five or more friends and colleagues. I continued to serve as a bartender, but we soon had to draft a neighbor's daughter to help serve the food. Then, as the crowd expanded further, we enlisted the help of a caterer. He was Windsor Jordan, who had assumed the management of his mother's legendary business after her death.[73]

Windsor brought his own kind of panache to the job. Wearing his *toque blanche*, he would pull into our driveway with his small crew a couple of hours before the appointed time of the party. His bartender was always the same—Mr. Dixon, a friendly but dignified Baptist church deacon who himself had never imbibed a drop of alcohol. After all the arrangements were in place, Windsor and I would pour ourselves a libation and gossip until party time. The most interesting conversations involved his tales of visiting his famous brother, Vernon (sometimes known as President Clinton's best friend) in Washington.

By the second time around, Windsor had converted the party into one that suited his taste. Although he generally would follow the menu upon which we had agreed, he also enjoyed surprising us by showing up with a special pâté or an elegant dessert. Nor was he completely satisfied with our guest list; we got used to him informing us that he had invited "a few people you need to get to know." And they showed up too!

After Windsor closed the business, we made another change. Now we prepare several dishes and invite all guests who so desire to bring "finger food" to share. The result is a five-hour, unending parade of regularly changing and delicious homemade dishes. Linda's niece, Allen, supervises the genial chaos, and bartending duties are handled by her husband, Lance, or another friend.

The final alteration to party protocol occurred the year that the celebration coincided with a warning from the weather department that an ice storm was headed our way. Atlantans take these kinds of alerts with excessive seriousness. When snow flurries are spotted in Birmingham, Alabama (two hours to the west of us) many folks race to the store for bread and batteries, and the education authorities begin shutting down our schools. Thus, it was no surprise when

---

73 Mary Jordan, founder of her eponymous catering company, carved herself a place in Atlanta history by serving the hospitality needs of Atlanta's elite families for decades.

our expected guests began calling to learn whether the party was still scheduled. I resolutely held the line and promised that we were made of stern stuff: the bar would open at 7 p.m. and the festivities would proceed as usual.

However, as the forecast worsened and the frequency of phone calls increased, I stifled my own hubris. To the extent possible, I notified everyone on the guest list that the party would begin at 4 p.m. and end by 9 p.m.

Our friends clearly were in a mood to celebrate. The first guests (mainly the older generation) arrived just before four o'clock, and they were followed by a steady stream of others. Most of them left by nine o'clock, and some of them encountered a few ice flurries, but all arrived home safely. When we conducted our postmortem of the event, we calculated that about half of the folks on the invitation list had braved the threatening weather and risked attendance.

The experience demonstrated that our older friends (people of our age, as we were forced to admit) preferred coming to the gala earlier and leaving earlier—although to be sure, we still have guests who help to open the bar and stay until or beyond closing time.

We happily accept the tributes from many that it may well be the best social occasion of the year. Part of the reason for that praise is that the date arrives after people have recovered from the Christmas holiday madness but still are ready for one more blast. We think another reason has to do with the rich variety of the guest list.

As should be clear, I am somewhat of a fanatic when it comes to the matter of promoting racial and other diversity. It's not simply a matter of morality or civility. I like my life to be interesting, so I have become distinctly uncomfortable in monochromatic settings. I can think of few more boring situations than to be in a room or a neighborhood full of old, white, straight, middle-class men like me with similar backgrounds and opinions. Seeing oneself in the mirror gets mighty tiresome.

I also like to be as knowledgeable as possible about what's happening in the world around me. If I'm not getting an African American or, for that matter, Latin American or Asian-American perspective on a situation, I am probably operating with insufficient information. If gay humor sails over my head or I'm not aware of legal threats to marginalized people, my awareness of my surroundings is incomplete. Over the years, I've discovered that limited knowledge is not the best foundation for good judgment.

Furthermore, by looking for opportunities to meet and spend time with different people, I've learned that all races and nationalities and people of differing sexual persuasions include folks with varying personalities. That discovery has freed me to make value judgments about them that don't have to rely upon either ignorance or guilt. If someone is a genius, I can proclaim her to be a genius, no matter what her color or native origin. By the same token, if someone is a sorry "sumbitch," then, regardless of his pigmentation or accent or place on the sexual spectrum, he's still a sorry "sumbitch."

To be sure, this approach isn't an especially gracious or noble way to confront the situation, and it is certainly lacking in theological or ethical integrity. However, I personally have found it to be refreshingly liberating.

The global pandemic resulted in the cancellation of Twelfth Night 2021. However, when it recurs, it will be another great success. Black and white and Asian and Hispanic guests will appear. Gay singles and couples will be present, and there also may be a few infants and nonagenarians in attendance. Even if what's going on is not an example of the Beloved Community for which good friends like John Lewis worked and prayed, we think it's a reasonable and worthy step in the right direction.

No Place Like Home

Linda and I remain in stubborn denial of the possibility that the day will come when we must vacate the property that has been the site of many Twelfth Night celebrations—as well as pig roasts, board meetings, birthday parties, fundraisers, weddings, and wedding receptions.

We also recognize that we're being naïve. Our mental, and probably our physical, conditions will eventually make it difficult if not impossible to function in our current abode. Here's just one example of what I mean: The other day (a concept of time that can embrace anything from yesterday to more than a year ago), I was composing an email to a friend. In it I was describing the deteriorating mental state of a mutual colleague. Halfway into the narrative, I found myself at a loss for the word I needed to describe the situation. Try as I might, I could not bring it into focus. After stubbornly struggling for several minutes and even intentionally distracting myself by a trip to the kitchen for . . . (I forget what it was) . . . I finally conceded that my brain wasn't going to cooperate. I punched out a synonym for the word I couldn't remember on the keyboard and requested help from the computer. A split second later, I had my answer. The word I couldn't recall was "dementia." Clearly, the shift into senility should be an easy transition for me.

One obvious first step would be to begin the search for a retirement community (something we used to call an "old folks' home" when I was a boy). The number of places in which we might take up residence is legion. The South is sprinkled (no, make that suffused) with a steadily expanding variety of opportunities for assisted senior living. The spread of these communities is helped in no small measure by the avalanche of Northern citizens who have been attracted southward by the allegedly warmer weather we enjoy down here. And the growing range of amenities they offer is mind-boggling.

The pressure to decide upon what might become our final home is no longer the idle question it once may have been. **Growing numbers of friends have moved into or reserved spaces in these gilded cages.** It's becoming more difficult to escape the questions from them and from family members about where Linda and I plan to go should we leave the only residence I have ever owned.

Now and then we make a half-hearted attempt to consider the matter seriously. The metro Atlanta area offers a wide variety of opportunities for senior living, and we've read through their printed materials. We've even toured one such facility—a gem of pristine lawns, paved pathways for walking and golf carts, various housing options, activity rooms, an indoor swimming pool, and a gym.

The entire property seemed to be fastidiously tended. Admittedly, it might be nice to be able to call for quick assistance if a tree limb fell on our roof or if a passing driver threw an empty beer can or Popeye's container on our front lawn. Then again, as Linda is fond of noting, neither of us has ever lived in a hygienic setting before; why start now?

We also do not find it encouraging to be told about all the activities available (we already have plenty to do) or, as one resident noted, the many committees on which our presence would be welcome.

Let me stop beating around the bush and explain a major obstacle to our relocation. Coming from the neighborhood where we live, I was immediately struck by the sheer "whiteness" of the compound we visited. Except for a few staff members, everybody we saw was thoroughly Caucasian. I finally asked our tour guide about the extent of racial variety among the residents. Her reply was that one of their "guests" was a veteran of the Tuskegee Air Men. It didn't take a lot of calculating for me to figure out that the African American gentleman in question would probably be dead by the time I ever got around to seeking admission. Further inquiries suggest strongly that other retirement clusters are also deficient on the diversity scale.

Our current home is across the street from an elementary school, and some of our neighbors have young offspring. The backgrounds of our lives include the sight and noise of small children—a seldom heard sound in retirement gulags. Instead, one is more likely to be subjected to the sound of other old people complaining about the meals and the frequent arrival of an ambulance or hearse to cart away one of those food critics.

Perhaps we will have found an ideal next-to-final destination by the time I compose another book. In the meantime, we will continue to love living in the house, the neighborhood, the city, and the region that form our home.

I hope to have made clear that, like the folks who produce *The Bitter Southerner*,[74] I love where I live, but I long for an "even better South." If our often-recalcitrant region can set the pace for new levels of civility and justice, then there is hope for the entire country. W.E.B. DuBois said, "As the South goes, so goes the nation." I choose to believe that his statement can support a positive interpretation.

As I'm finishing this manuscript, a worldwide pandemic and pernicious economic and other inequities rooted in racism and xenophobia continue to threaten the soul of our country. It remains to be seen whether these deadly phenomena have the potential to encourage or perhaps frighten us into better and more constructive behavior. All of us bear a measure of responsibility for addressing and, Lord willing, even helping to erase these offenses.

The sketches that I have written and collected in this volume clearly do not constitute a complete picture of the South, nor are they intended to be a guidebook to a better way of living in our region. However, in their own way, I hope that they may serve as reminders that we are best served when we humbly accept the truth of who we have been, recognize the delight that diversity can offer, and resolve to embrace a vision of a world in which we all are worthy of each other's understanding and compassion.

---

74 *The Bitter Southerner* is a weekly digital publication which declares that its single aim is "to uncover the American South in all of its truth and complexity."

About the Author

MARTIN LEHFELDT was born in New York City, raised in Camden, New Jersey, and attended Quaker institutions from Moorestown Friends School through Haverford College. Strongly encouraged to follow his grandfather and father into the Lutheran ministry despite a desire to become a journalist, he earned a Master of Divinity at Union Theological Seminary in New York—but then "self-defrocked" in the mid-1960s. The opportunity to direct a program that recruited and placed outstanding young faculty members at historically Black colleges throughout the South gave him a unique perspective on that region and lured him to Atlanta. What was intended to be a brief sojourn blossomed into a career as a college development officer, a fundraising consultant, and President of the Southeastern Council of Foundations. During five decades as a "naturalized" Southerner traveling widely in the region, he has become known as a speaker and author whose books include *The Sacred Call, Notes from a Non-Profitable Life*, and (with Jamil Zainaldin) *The Liberating Promise of Philanthropy*.

CPSIA information can be obtained
at www.ICGtesting.com
Printed in the USA
LVHW051556221022
731329LV00006B/250